To Len With love, [signature] '/90

Gentle Words In A Raging Storm

Prayers for all occasions

By Gary R. Weaver

C.S.S. Publishing Company, Inc.
Lima, Ohio

GENTLE WORDS IN A RAGING STORM

Copyright © 1991 by
The C.S.S. Publishing Company, Inc.
Lima, Ohio

Library of Congress Cataloging-in-Publication Data
Weaver, Gary R., 1945-
    Gentle words in a raging storm: prayers for all occasions / by
Gary R. Weaver.
        p.   cm.
    ISBN 1-55673-288-0
    1. Prayers.   I. Title.
BV²45.W35   1991
242'.8—dc20   90-47310
                                                                         CIP

9121 / ISBN 1-55673-288-0   PRINTED IN U.S.A.

To my counselor, critic and best friend, whose daily
life is a living prayer, Kathleen . . .

Contents

Foreword

About 20 years ago I attended a church meeting in Coolidge, Arizona. Some 200 believers showed up for a quarterly meeting of Presbytery, one of those essential yet routine events, which mark life in the mainstream churches. The agenda frequently flirted with the boring, interrupted with aimless, mindless discussion that so often monopolizes the direction of the organizational church today.

At last it was lunch time. A decent meal and lively conversation restored our humor and humanity. During dessert, with a second glass of ice tea, it was announced that a dramatic presentation would follow. I don't recall the theme or title or even the author. It was something by T. S. Eliot or Christopher Fry, written by someone competent to link religion and the arts. Most of the audience, like myself, stayed for the program presented in the church dining room.

The actors were local church members, well versed, and the one-act play which followed was far beyond anyone's expectations. As I said, I can't recall the playwright, title or theme, but Gary Weaver was one of the players and for interpretation and intensity, he hit a home run.

Since that moment in a church dining room in a desert town of Arizona, I have followed with interest, and at times, excitement, the career of the Rev. Gary Weaver. Sometimes I have seen the actor, more often the activist. The educator appeared, then the counselor, teacher, pastor, the dreamer, the preacher. For me, Weaver's life is a living example of our need for adventure being as great as our need for security.

And Weaver has lots of nerve. To propose a prayer book. And the audacity as well to ask someone to publish them. Are we in the same century? Is this an era of prayer, devotions, and claims of the heart?

Somehow Weaver discovered a fearless publisher to join him in this dangerous enterprise and here at the start I want to salute both of them for the daring creativity to present a volume of prayers in a disbelieving day.

I think I am right on this: the religious mood of the hour is not centered on prayer, the concerns of the inner life, the desire for a sustained conversation with the Spirit of God. The public reflection of faith, as interpreted by the media church, is highly pro-active, constantly agitated by motion and color and noise. There is little evidence of the electronic clergy's interest in the pursuit of a quiet time, periods of silence, a willingness to wait upon the Lord. The prayers of the congregation are so far off camera as to be non-existent. The observance and sharing of the sacraments? They simply fail to fit into the time bites of television's religious entertainment. Is Weaver in the right century?

However, the more we examine the life of the spirit and the authentic requirements of faith, the more we discover our dependence on the life of prayer and the habits of praying people. The whole sweep of Scripture reinforces this view: Moses on his knees as he confronts the holiness of God in the burning bush of the Sinai desert. Samuel, Solomon, and the Psalmists remind us of the closeness of a caring God in prayer. Jesus' ministry beginning in the solitude of the wilderness and ending with the conversations of the Upper Room and the petitions of the Garden of Gethsemane — all surrounded and sustained by prayer with God.

In his helpful book, *The Road To Daybreak*, Henri Nouwen correctly calls the mood of believing people when he says,

> *Too often in religion the moral life gets all the attention, and so we are in danger of forgetting the crucial importance of the mystical life, which is the life of the heart.*

In my college years at Wooster, the moral urgencies of the day were vividly presented in class and in convocation. Norman Thomas, addressing the dilemmas of the Cold War, drew one of the largest audiences ever. Yet one of the enduring presentations that now captures my thinking (made to a smaller, more select group) was the appearance of Rufus Jones, the great Quaker leader and mystic who within himself and manner, reflected the grace and joy of the Holy Spirit.

In Gary Weaver's public prayers we sense the balance of silence and action, solitude and social concern. Actually, many aspects of Weaver's personality would lead you to look for the mystical and the pious somewhere else. He is active in almost every outdoor sport, participates constantly in team activities and has always been of imposingly powerful stature. His several years of public school teaching prior to ordination gave him the experience of teaching and leading youth on a daily basis. Such a life would seem external, social, and highly interactive on an hour-to-hour basis.

Yet another personality development is just as marked: the interest in the quiet dialogue of a professional counselor; the longer preparation for an advanced degree; the listening skills; the patience and forbearance with people with heavy hearts and deep pain. All this is the chemistry which creates a compelling prayer life and makes possible a volume of *Gentle Words In A Raging Storm.*

During an especially tense time of our shared ministry in New Mexico, with terrorism overseas and natural disasters at home, Gary offered this corporate prayer which for many, blended public compassion and private concern:

O God of all precious things,
Who hears our pain even when tears block our words,
Create in us a heart of laughter and hope.

May your Spirit of comfort strengthen the families of trapped miners or the victims of senseless bombings;

May it still the anxiety of those who live with enormous pressure and stress;

May it fill the emptiness of lost and lonely lives.

As I read again the focus and intensity of this morning public prayer and how it incorporated the feelings of helplessness and rage of so many present, I am more impressed than ever of the mature theology that shaped the next petition which followed:

And yet, we know your comforting spirit does not feed an empty stomach, nor insist on the end of war and fighting,
nor free the politically oppressed.

Only your Spirit of love which confronts and changes the hearts of people everywhere can do that.

So bring us comfort where we need comfort
but where we need justice, let there be love.

In some case worshipers thought this was a soft landing to a harsh and unbearable condition, Gary continued in that prayer:

Let us never be content with murder, tyranny, starvation, pollution or any form of human cruelty.
May we continue to groan and lift loud voices to those who can effect political change;

But even more, may we lift our hands or bend our backs or use our minds to help those in distress — who stand at our doorsteps, or live down the block or huddle in isolated areas of the city.

O Suffering and Compassionate God, hear our prayers as we continue to trust in that Spirit that leads us away from arrogance and self-satisfaction toward a life of forgiveness, humility, and growth.

That prayer, fresh as this morning, written 15 years ago, reveals the timelessness of our faith in the expression of one who believes and has the capacity to lead others in a mutual pilgrimage.

Over the last half century there have been some important titles published in this field. One thinks of the highly popular work, *The Prayers of Peter Marshall,* which recorded his invocations for the U.S. Senate. An essential volume for many Christians has been the *Diary of Private Prayer* by John Baille, which appeared around mid-century. These were followed by Harry Emerson Fosdick's *A Book of Public Prayer.* Fosdick's prayers and litanies are as arresting and inspirational as his sermons. In the introduction to his book, he admits to some anxiety shared with other "non-liturgical traditions" over the use of printed prayers.

Nevertheless, Dr. Fosdick decided to challenge the notion of "non-liturgical churches" that to be genuine, "a prayer should be spontaneous and extempore."

The pastor of Riverside Church, New York had reached a different conclusion, notwithstanding his own Baptist ordination:

The emphasis on spontaneity, however, neglects the important fact that leading a congregation in public prayer is a work of art, demanding expert skill and painstaking preparation.

We must recognize that many of Weaver's prayers not only will be appreciated by others but will be used by many as well. This creates a certain kind of ecclesiastical theft that borders on the dishonest, since liturgists rarely give timely reference to their sources. My larger hope is that this book, in its material, form, and theme will encourage many to honor Gary's effort by writing carefully their own prayers inspired by his discipline and faithfulness.

Gentle Words In A Raging Storm is a hopeful sign that there is a serious move within the Christian community to reclaim the integrity of worship. The New Testament admonishes us to do things "decently and in order." The craftsmanship of our sermons and the design and composition of our prayers fit closely with the revival of the use of the lectionary. Yet the use of the more formal liturgy remind us how quickly we need to add original petitions within the Sunday use of the traditional.

My colleague in ministry, The Rev. Linda Roberts, recalls for us in one of her poems, that the daily and frequent habits of existence need not be tired and cliche-driven:

I will mark this day with a white stone . . . like the one you gave me and remember the clean light of mornings, the precision of peeled oranges and coffee;
The perfection of the ordinary that escapes history like an unsung psalm.

Gary Weaver represents the ranks of dynamic prayer people, who coax others to a higher, better way. These pages contain flashes of truth tested in the hand-to-hand combat of life and in that contest, we are wonderfully reminded of the Winner . . .   .

David Poling

Preface

Prayer is a strange genre. It is part poetry, part free-association and part love letter to God. When spoken, it is the most intimate, sacred speech we utter. When written down, it becomes a diary of the heart, a journal of our innermost feelings, fears, hopes, desires. It is a full disclosure of a person's thoughts, values, faith — a complete confession!

Any wonder, then, that I would hesitate to have them published, these fragments of my inner life? On the other hand, prayer insists on being shared. It may come from the individual; it belongs to the community. When he taught us to pray, Jesus told us to say, "Our Father . . ." not "**My** Father." From the very first, prayer became inclusive, plural, something for the "two or three who gather" in his name to say together.

I wrote these prayers to be inclusive, to include you and me in their references, and to be public, used for any occasion where people listen for the leader's prayer to guide their own meditation. They were written from the heart, from the heat of my passion for people in their honest struggle with life, love and faith in God. They were written so we could pray together. So, let us pray . . . .

Gary R. Weaver

Acknowledgments

It is true that writing is a lonely profession. It is also true that we never enter solitude alone. We always carry with us an interior assembly of voices — the voices of family and friends who influence our thoughts and our prayers. I am grateful to that whole assembly who encourage and inform me but I have space to mention only a few: R. Ray Atchison, Ila Joy Weaver, Ann Ladd, David Poling, Malcolm Boyd, Roberta Courtney Meyers.

I appreciate my two daughters who are in my prayers daily: Lisa and Angie.

These prayers have all been "field tested" in the churches I have served over 18 years so I want to acknowledge and thank them: Community Presbyterian, Coolidge, Arizona; First Presbyterian, Albuquerque, New Mexico; Westmont Presbyterian, Johnstown, Pennsylvania; Wasatch Presbyterian, Salt Lake City, Utah.

Finally, I want to mention my gratitude for the special support of Walter and Helen Kershaw.

Acknowledgments

Teach Us To Pray (1)

O God of Love, we ask you to teach us to pray.
What we really mean is teach us to believe in prayer,
the power of prayer:
to believe that our concerns and hopes,
our fears and frustrations
when lifted up to your ear
are heard;
to believe that you not only hear
but act to soothe our troubled souls,
to bring about relief and restoration,
to provide us with courage and confidence beyond our
expectations.
O Lord, teach us to believe in the activity of your
love in our lives,
to believe you are constantly working with us to
perfect our ability to love as you love us
and to believe you catch us when we fall.
O Lord, who teaches us to hold on to the faith we
have been given, no matter how small,
teach us not only to pray
but to believe in the mysterious power of prayer.
Amen.

Teach Us To Pray (2)

Great God of Life,
you are the one Christ called, "Father,"
the one to whom he prayed when his loneliness was
unbearable or the demands of this life were beyond
his human strength.
As the disciples of old asked him, so we ask you,
"Lord, teach us to pray."
Teach us to pray for those who encounter one tragic
circumstance after another and ask us, "Why?"
Teach us to pray for those who have lost too many
struggles and want to regain their will to fight on
and ask us, "How?"
Teach us to pray for those who ask us nothing
and seem lost in their addiction or self-absorption.
Teach us to pray for the very old who are confined
to beds or attached to machines or live with constant
pain.
Teach us to pray for families crippled by
misunderstanding, vengeance or violence.
Teach us to pray for those who walk the streets alone,
not knowing where they are going or why.
And teach us to pray for ourselves
that we may learn to love more,
listen more and
pray more together. Amen.

Teach Us To Pray (3)

O God on high, our concerns are many and continuous.
With each passing day we hear of another friend who
needs a special petition of prayer.
We arise in the morning and open our newspaper to
headlines that echo the screams of a world in need
of prayer.
When we come home to our families, tired, fatigued,
unable to listen to the hurts of our children,
we need your prayer.
So we ask, O Lord, that you teach us to pray.
We know you do not need to hear our prayers to be
responsive toward the sick, hurting, alone and fearful.
You do not have to be asked to do that which you do
already.
Rather, teach us how our prayer helps us align our
desires to your purposes,
how naming our concerns helps us to join you in acting
on them,
how giving voice to the groans of our soul helps
relieve the burden we have been carrying alone.
Encourage us to believe prayer matters,
that you listen,
that even in our praying your love is becoming active
through us in the world. Amen.

Teach Us To Pray (4)

Holy God, we ask for your protection from the pain
of life;
you give us the maturity to face it.
We ask for riches and wealth;
you give us the richness of wisdom, the wealth of
generosity.
We ask for happiness and good times;
you send us strength for our sorrows.
We ask for sunshine;
you give us your Son.
O God, we are thankful you do not give us all we ask
but only what we need.
May we become your children without becoming childish.
May our faith continually be informed by our minds
as well as our sentiments.
May our obedience to your way
not become a dependency of mindless discipleship
but a commitment that remains alert and discerning.
May we be wise as foxes and innocent as lambs,
so that we can live in this world and remain effective
without losing our dream of love and faithfulness.
O Lord, hear the prayers of our lips
and the prayers of our hearts. Amen.

Personal Prayer (1)

How like me to go off to write a book of prayers
and forget to pray.
And how like you, O Lord, to smile at that
knowing me better than I know myself.
How seldom do I find the time,
make the time,
take the time
to spend time with you?
How often do you come to me
tugging at my shirt sleeve,
bumping into my heart,
nudging at my conscience?
I don't know if it's prayer,
but we do communicate
don't we?
We do find a way to keep in touch,
to stay together,
to move through each day with hope,
to sing a song of love,
to enter stumbling, shaking
into the suffering of another.
It's a way of praying continuously,
constantly, with each trembling thought,
each warm desire,
to do it your way,
to follow where you lead,
to go where you send me. Amen.

Personal Prayer (2)

O Silent and Mysterious God, forgive my doubts and
impatience.
For I sometimes yearn for a loud, aggressive God:
one who will shame the thoughtless and humiliate the
proud with his strong arm of power.
And sometimes I want to know the secret of all things
and to demand a justification for the things I don't
understand.
I want a reason for chilling winters that slay the
sick and old;
I insist on an explanation for the sudden dismantling
of a relationship through death or disloyalty;
I seek to know why children flirt with drug addiction
or become enslaved to alcohol;
I wonder why the mean, callous and cunning always
seem to come out on top, while the winsome, kind and
decent people die in the prime of life;
and I want to know why people must so often suffer
the last years of their lives alone or incapacitated.
I want answers!
. . . not faith.
I want a puppet who jumps to the yank of my
indignation, not a God who calls me to obedience and
faithfulness.
Restore within me a humble and contrite heart,
faith in your wisdom, acceptance of your will
and trust in the ultimate purpose and aim of a God
who shows his power in powerlessness by allowing
his only Son to become the victim of hatred, prejudice
and pride — all in the name of love.
Forgive me, Great God of Life, for entertaining false
gods and make me ever thankful for the living witness
of our Lord Jesus Christ. Amen.

Personal Prayer (3)

Deliver me, O God, from my self-imposed limitations.
Deliver me from that which keeps me down or holds
me back,
from that which chips away at my self-confidence,
from that which obstructs or aborts the birth of your
gift of life and hope in my heart.
May I find the courage to release the powers within,
to throw off the shackles of shame and timidity,
to walk with faith instead of fear.
May I dare to become what you created me to be
and to strive always for "the more excellent way."
May the word, "Yes," replace my, "Not yet;"
the affirmation, "All things are possible with God,"
dislodge my rationalizations, my clinging to the
familiar, the safe, the well-worn.
O God, who makes all things new, transform my
trembling will into the smiling confidence of one
who lives not for oneself but for your Son, Jesus
Christ our Lord, in whose name I pray. Amen.

Personal Prayer (4)

God of Grace, when I stumble I look for your hand.
I shudder in my loneliness and feel cut off from your community,
But I cannot hide from your pursuing, persistent love.
Where can I flee from your presence?
In the darkest corner of the earth, you are there.
Thank you, God, for seeking me out, for refusing to permit my guilt, my shame, my sin to rule my life.
When I hide my hurt and cut off my pain from my consciousness, you open the wound,
let the poison drain and apply a healing balm.
I, who am a half-person searching for wholeness, integrity and peace, discover in your warm acceptance my holiness and self-worth.
I thank you, God, that in becoming one with Christ I become one with myself.
His Spirit completes my personality, fills my emptiness, rubs smooth the rough spots of my selfishness, self-justification, pride, prejudice and fear.
Your Spirit opens up my tight spaces to feel the freedom of the skies,
the hope of the morning sun,
the joy of the after-rain color.
Father of my faith, Mother of my life, friend and Lord, hear my prayer! Amen.

Personal Prayer (5)

It's been good to spend the day with you, Lord,
to admire your arching red rock
emerging from the desert,
to experience for myself
what others told me.
The telling may be good,
the experience better!
How grateful I am, Lord, that you gave us
more than story.
You gave us yourself!
You came to me in the shadow of my awareness,
in the darkness of my doubt,
in the endless abyss of my fear.
You have become for me an undeniable presence
a reliable friend,
the one who walks in
when the rest of the world
walks away. Amen.

Prayers Of The Morning (1)

O Lord of Life,
out of the night the new day is given.
We wake to its call.
The day is announced in the dusty, red light of dawn.
It spreads out before us your secret gifts and mystery.
May we approach each day with great expectation,
the courage to ask and to explore,
the love to
not only receive its gifts
but to pass them on.
May we participate in the movement of your
self-giving Spirit
which holds nothing for itself
but produces life in the giving.
Like the clouds that absorb the mist
only to return it to the earth
as generous drops of rain,
so may we receive your Spirit
which magnifies our own
and which when given away
satisfies the thirst of body and soul.
Like your sun
which burns constantly to provide light,
may we with inflamed hearts
let your light so shine
that the blind may see
and the lost may find a place of
safety and warmth. Amen.

Prayers Of The Morning (2)

O God of Light,
who makes the sun to rise each morning,
we praise you for your Son Jesus,
who came into the world to bring the light of life
to a darkened world.
By the light of his love,
the shadowy recesses of our lives,
the pitch-black corners of our souls
are exposed and robbed of their power to frighten
or imprison us with their sinister secrets.
So we find our lives renewed, our hope restored,
our faith given new meaning and direction.
May his light be shed in those lives still trapped
by darkness where suffering and oppression
overcloud each moment
as if to deny the reality of his love.
And may his light illuminate our paths
so we will see the way to follow. Amen.

Prayers Of The Morning (3)

O God of china-blue skies and dazzling sunrises,
we wake to a new day filled with promise and
possibility.
Help us to see beyond what is to what can be.
Help us to look beyond the difficulties of the goal
you set before us and to focus on the dream.
Help us to do our very best at work, in the home,
in the world
and to build a community of love and reconciliation
wherever we live.
May we not be satisfied with second best,
the easiest path,
the familiar and the safe.
Grant us the boldness to lift lazy will
out of the stupor of security
to the risk of faith,
the joy of service,
the laughter of love. Amen.

Prayers Of The Morning (4)

Great God of the Morning,
with each new day your promise of hope is restored;
in every sunrise we see your face.
Each day is like the first day you created
with the same invitation for us to live in your image,
to work creatively and obediently.
Each day is like the Day of Resurrection
filled with new life and hope.
The darkest night fades into the light of the morning.
So why, O Lord, do we doubt?
Where is our faith?
We have a daily reminder of your faithfulness
and yet we cling to darkness.
We continue to wonder if you hear our prayers,
see our tears, feel our suffering.
When we send our painful groans into the heavens,
we hear nothing but the echo of our own voices.
When people we love drift into death,
our grief turns to rage and cynicism;
we think you do not care!
What little faith we have, O God.
How senseless our skepticism.
Sprinkle us with your love, Great Gardener,
so our mustard-seed faith will grow like large elms
whose leafy arms stretch to the heavens,
and arch in prayer.
Give us the faith of the rising sun,
the trust of the trees,
the hope that springs eternal from constant prayer.
Amen.

Prayers For Courage And Hope (1)

O God of Hope,
the turbulent waters of life wear us out.
Our arms are sore, our breath gone; we can swim
no more.
It seems often to be just that moment you choose
to invite us to walk on the water,
to do the impossible,
to go beyond what we think we can do,
to risk the unknown, the unfamiliar, the unexpected.
We are, like Peter, humans of little faith.
We may puff it up so that it supports us for awhile,
but then our faces turn blue and we blow it out
with exhausted relief!
Teach us to learn our limitations so that we will
call on your unlimited power.
Take from us our indignation and arrogance and give
us the humble but uplifting power of acceptance.
Show us, when we forget, the strength that comes from
relationship, from community, from a helping hand.
May we be open to your creative activity in our lives
which introduces new options,
paints with bright colors,
dances to a different tune.
We are all handicapped by our fear, our lack of faith.
Save us, O Lord, from sinking in courage,
from drowning in our despair.
Give us your hand and we will walk with you,
even upon the waters! Amen.

Prayers For Courage And Hope (2)

Up from the underneath we come, O God,
up from the agony of guilt,
    the gulf of loneliness,
    the paralysis of fear,
    the emptiness of sorrow
into the warm light of day,
into the light of truth and forgiveness,
reassurance and comfort,
celebration and joy.
Our days are clouded by timid souls, trite sayings,
false promises and prophets of doom.
How grateful we are for the clear, ringing voice of
the children of God,
people of faith and real hope,
people who do not shrink before a challenge but ignite
others with their persistent trust in God.
How thankful we are for people who love easily, quietly
and universally all who call upon their concern.
How blessed we are for people who look beyond their
own suffering long enough to see the hurt of others,
who courageously leave their own loneliness to embrace
the lonely,
who quiet their own doubts by comforting the fear
of others,
who look to you with an undying, indestructible
conviction of hope.
Thank you, Lord, for the courage of ordinary people
who inspire our own. Amen.

Prayers For Courage And Hope (3)

O God, who sees into our hearts,
you know how we struggle for dignity,
how we work for self-esteem.
And you know how fragile we are in courage and
confidence.
Perhaps the world IS too much with us!
We are keenly aware of its warring hatred, insatiable
greed, strutting pride . . .
and we get caught up in it
making its values our own.
In fear we abandon our faith in the power of love
and bow before the missiles of madness.
In self-contempt we ignore your forgiveness and seek
to prove ourselves worthy,
to justify our mistakes and acts of stupidity
and defend our devotion to prestige and wealth.
Give us the courage to work creatively for peace
in ourselves, our homes, our nation and in the world.
Give us the confidence to be self-sacrificing instead
of self-expanding,
to give ourselves away to others,
to enjoy the generous expression of your love.
And give us faith to see beyond sight and sensibility
a vision of your kingdom on earth — the kingdom of
the heart. Amen.

Prayers For Courage And Hope (4)

O Lord, how we seek to be faithful
and yet how we are easily distracted from your vision.
We are so impatient with your promise of new life.
We want it now, not tomorrow.
We want it for ourselves, not just for our neighbors.
We want the triumph of Easter without the tragedy
of Good Friday.
We want the prize without the race.
Give strength to our fainting heart,
courage to our fading will,
faith to our shattered hope.
May we seek your way and not our own.
May we discover your kingdom in self-sacrifice,
instead of building our kingdom through
self-gratification.
May we not seek happiness but joy.
May we not seek the detachment of pleasure
but the painful involvement in the suffering of others.
May we not expect life to be fair
but may we strive for justice.
May we trust you to take care of us
while we pledge ourselves to caring for others.
For this is the faith we seek,
to which we have been called
and for which we have been born anew in that Spirit
who keeps us faithful. Amen.

Prayers For Courage And Hope (5)

In the eye of the storm
we hear your gentle words, O Lord.
Though the earth trembles,
though the tempest of human strife rages on,
your calming Spirit speaks of hope.
You show us how a heart filled with your
forgiving love has no room for hatred, vengeance
and violence.
Drenched in the waters of our baptism,
nourished by the bread of life,
healed by the cup of salvation,
quieted by your still, small voice
we can walk in the thunder,
dance like daisies in the rain,
soar through the flash of lightning
and look for the coming of the sun.
Forgive our languid faith,
the fear that submits to false security
and turns away from the source of life.
Help us hang on to that which is true,
the only one who can create life out of death,
new life in the old,
life that lasts,
our Lord, Jesus Christ.
May we, like Jesus,
face all peril with a prayer,
a prayer that has power to restore
our sinking souls. Amen.

Prayers For Deliverance (1)

Teach us to know your patience, O God, and to trust
your deliverance.
May nothing in this life keep us from believing in
your saving, steadfast love.
May nothing enslave our spirit of hope:

> not pain or persecution;
> not suffering and disease;
> not separation or divorce;
> not the loss of loved ones;
> not even the imminence of our own death.

May nothing on earth nor anything in our imaginations
keep us from the confidence of our faith in your
goodness.
Set our feet on solid ground, O God.
Help us remember our own lives and all the little
deliverances you have provided.
Put a new song in our mouths that we may sing with
joy of your kindness and mercy.
We would ask to be saved from suffering, O Lord, but
if not, then from the slavery of suffering,
the clinging captivity of fear,
the awesome abyss of our sorrow and grief.
When we fall, give us faith to trust that you will
be there to catch us and to walk with us out of the
valley of death to the pinnacle of new life.
Good Shepherd, lead your sheep
when we are able to follow.
But when we get lost, find us;
when wounded, heal us;
when we grow weary, carry us in your arms.
Amen.

Prayers For Deliverance (2)

O Saving God, we thank you for the grace in which
we participate and for the redemptive activity of
your Spirit working in us and for us.
Save us, O Lord, from fear:
>   fear of failure and fear of success;
>   fear of death and fear of life;
>   fear of tragedy and grief;
>   fear of joy and laughter.

May we become aware of that perfect love which casts
out fear — the love of our Lord Jesus Christ.
It is love that dares to make amends, restore
communication, forget the past and move forward into
a new, creative relationship.
It is love that makes enemies friends.
It is love that does not rejoice when others stumble
but generously celebrates the success of others.
It is love that refuses a posture of superiority or
a position of inferiority but enjoys what makes us
different and what makes us one.
It is love that chooses affirmation of people over
acquisition of things; giving over taking; advocacy
of the powerless over adoration of the powerful.
It is love that casts out fear and clears a place
for faith to grow.
Thank you, God, for sending this love into all the
world so the world would not perish in fear but live
in faith. Amen.

Prayers For Deliverance (3)

O Great God of Hope, we come to you when our lives
are broken and torn, when our hope is vanquished and our
faith is small.
We come to you when once-cherished relationships are
lost to death or dissipated by distance, time,
misunderstanding or neglect.
We come to you when our body and mind have become
captives of a destructive addiction, when courage
and will have been replaced by a bottle, a drug or
emotional dependency.
We come to you when the promise of the "good life"
has been found lacking, when clothes and cuisine,
cars and cappucino become insufficient nourishment
for the hunger of the human spirit.
We come to you because we have nowhere else to go,
because all of our attempts to create wholeness and
health apart from you have been futile and trite,
filled with the clanging gong of slogans and the
symbols of success — signifying nothing!
Save us from ourselves, O God: from self-absorption,
self-indulgence and self-idolization. Heal us from
the sickness of the body but even more from the
sickness of the soul.
May we get caught up in the current of your compassion,
the flood of your forgiveness and so lose ourselves
in the wide ocean of your love. Amen.

Prayers For Deliverance (4)

Great God of Justice and Mercy, we are shocked and
outraged at the continual litany of atrocities that
plague and pervert this planet!
We are sick hearing about another woman violated in
a grocery store parking lot;
we deplore the acts of terrorism and the terrible
acts of governmental forces against their own people;
we are distressed about child abuse, molestations,
killings and suicide.
In disgust and desperation we run to our rifles,
padlock our doors and windows and build bigger bombs.
But we have no assurance we are safe from harm's way.
Where can we flee from danger?
How can we escape the raging swirl of global insanity?
It is all about us.
It is within us!
O God, have mercy on us.
Save us from ourselves:
save us from the violence that lurks in our hearts;
save us from the delusion that power will protect
us.
Give us faith to see
beyond sound and fury
the kingdom that dwells within us,
the possibility of creative love,
the peace that comes from the gift of your hope.
Like Jesus, may we strive to be a stillness in the
storm.
May we be a calm presence in the hysteria of anger
informed by fear.
May we, like Christ, have the courage to employ self-
sacrifice instead of self-interest, thus discovering
at what great risk the commandment of love is to be
followed.
Certainly, with love there is no defense,
only the hope that, at last, the world will be
redeemed.
Amen.

Prayers For Deliverance (5)

O Liberating Lord, you call us out of captivity to
the freedom of the human spirit.
When our false faces and pretentious posturing shield
our honest feelings and shroud our secret fears,
you remind us that the truth shall set us free.
When we are bent over and burdened by the weight of
our selfish ambitions or the assumption of too much
responsibility,
you invite us to take your yoke upon us — the one that
is easy and light.
When the darkness of doubt and fear encircles us and
we become lost and confused,
you come to us with the announcement that you are
the Light of the World — a light which the darkness
has not and cannot overcome.
When we become victimized by our insatiable appetite
for pleasure and excitement,
you assure us that you alone are the Bread of Life
and that if we come to you and believe in you
we shall never hunger, never thirst.
O Lord, save us from ourselves!
We seem to compulsively prefer captivity to freedom.
We become complacent in the safety of our cells.
Forgive our grumbling and resistance and show us again
and again how the weighty wings of faith can lift
us to heaven
and to the heart of God. Amen.

Prayers For Deliverance (6)

O Lord, may your light burn within our hearts.
Lift our eyes from the seductive sleep of doubt and
despair.
Awaken us to the possibilities of faith believed and
lived out.
Give us the nerve to dare attempting the untried,
befriending the unloved,
forgiving the unpardonable.
So heavily do we load our lives with the luggage of
yesterday!
Free us from our boxes of blindness to see light in
the infinity of space.
Startle us out of the trance of timeless trouble to
the alert, blinking vision of your resurrected joy.
May the same eyes which so easily picture you nailed
to the cross
perceive you rising from the tomb.
May the same heart which can so easily remember past
pain, disappointment, failure, also warm with the
memory of past release, surprise and victory.
Give us faith to be your people of the Exodus, your
disciples of the Resurrection, your agents of
liberation and hope. Amen.

Prayers For Deliverance (7)

Faithful God, we move toward you
with timidity and doubt,
trusting you will allay our fears
and restore our confidence.
Sometimes it feels like the pain and disappointment
of this life is too much,
that it is more than we can bear,
that we will not survive.
Darkness overtakes us
and despair looms all around us.
And yet, we go on living, hoping and waiting . . .
until one day we notice the world is strikingly
beautiful;
that the simple trust and profound resilience of
children are conveyed in their curiosity, wonder and
laughter;
that we do have a choice to reach out for help
or to extend our love;
that we are forgiven and the past cannot contain us;
that each new day reveals surprising possibilities
and creative challenges;
that however discouraged, we were not destroyed,
however hurt, we were not defeated.
We did survive!
Resplendent God, we know that only you could design
a heart that not only pumps life blood into all the
body but also serves as the fountain of compassion,
the source of poet's dreams,
the origin of self-giving love,
the place of prayer.
Touch our hearts and make them whole.
Fill them with such boundless hope that our minds
will burst with gratitude and praise,
our mouths will shout with joy,
our hands will clap and our feet will dance!
For you are the Lord, Giver of Mercy,
whose love never fails and whose promises are sure.
Amen.

Prayers For Deliverance (8)

O Great Resurrection God,
this is the day you have made
and we rejoice in it!
For you have provided in your carefully crafted plan
a path to life eternal,
a way to endless love,
a means of renewing forgiveness.
O God of passion,
your sorrow is deeper than ours;
it seeps between our sadness and sickness,
beneath our grief and despair
and lifts us up.
Your love is greater than ours;
it follows us into death
falls with us through nothingness
and catches us in outstretched hands.
How unrelenting is your forgiveness;
it tracks us through the greedy hell of our own making;
it stalks us through the forest of our excuses, pride
and self-deceit;
it slips through the prison bars of our guilt
and sets us free.
Free to live with integrity!
Free to struggle for universal justice and peace.
Free to walk humbly with our Lord Jesus Christ. Amen.

Prayers For Personal Honesty (1)

God of gentle dreams and awesome space,
cultivate in our hearts a faith that is tall and sure.
In a frivolous and fake society that worships things
and preys on our fears,
we often feel confused and alone.
Create in us a spirit that overcomes hopelessness
without avoiding necessary grief,
that celebrates in spontaneous joy
without forced smiles and contrived entertainment,
that finds satisfaction in simplicity
without fearing the complex,
that accepts responsibility
without the burden of obligation.
No mind is without doubt
and we would not ask for that;
doubt has quickened our desire for truth
and prompted our search for purpose.
But we do ask for the hope of a spring rain,
the certainty of the sunrise,
the wonder of new growth,
the power of silence
and the peace which remains beyond expression,
yet never beyond your presence. Amen.

Prayers For Personal Honesty (2)

O God of Truth,
tear down our visages of pretense
that we may discover the joy of facing you just as
we are.
It is not that we have found you
but that you have found us hiding behind an endless
wall of excuses,
crouching in the shadow of doubt,
darting from our images of fear.
God of Hope,
teach us to overcome pain with prayer,
to conquer anxiety by facing our fears,
to rise above death with love and memory.
May your Spirit,
which recognizes we are different, yet the same,
reach inside our stone edifices and touch that
pulsating desire in us
to serve the God of Truth.
Father of the Friendless,
Creator of all that is good,
may that which you have given us to share with others
not be cheapened by our self-conceit,
nor obscured by our self-doubt.
Rather, may your gifts take on power and breadth
as we express them in loving commitment to your
lost and forgotten children,
in the name of the One who led us away from ourselves
and toward each other. Amen.

Prayers For Personal Honesty (3)

The tedium of banal chatter and senseless conflict
occupy too much of our time and energy, O God.
We want to come out from behind
the masks of pretension,
the walls of pride,
the aprons of fear,
the weapons of hate
and encounter each other with truth, forgiveness, love.
For we fear that life will pass and we will not
experience the fulfillment of
knowing and being known,
accepting and being accepted,
loving and being loved.
Give us courage to reach out,
to risk rejection and humiliation in hope of
making contact,
restoring communication
or finding a friend.
Fears of failure and the memory of
painful past attempts caution us
to quit trying,
to give up,
to stop trusting the possibility of love.
Help us to see this as the counsel of death,
loneliness, separation, helplessness.
May we believe enough in your Spirit of Grace to
risk the hurt of love
in order to find the joy of love. Amen.

Prayers For Healing And Forgiveness (1)

O Lord of Life,
we come to you with our sorrows, our heartaches,
our bodily and spiritual pain
asking for healing and help.
Often we want more than we receive
and overlook your constant healing activity in our
lives that works to return us
to life and hope, love and friendship,
caring and community.
O Lord, you come to us when we can no longer come
to you.
You speak to us when there are no more prayers in
our mouths or in our hearts.
When we cannot walk another step, when we tire of
being strong and brave, our legs give out,
we stumble and fall.
But you are there to catch us,
to hold us up until we regain strength enough
to stand on our own and walk again with hope.
We thank you, Lord, for the miracle of healing in
our hearts and for that love which stays with us
even when we let you down. Amen.

Prayers For Healing And Forgiveness (2)

Forgiving Father, Loving Lord,
help us to perceive the hypocrisy of hatred,
the self-destructive result of long-held resentments.
How our hostility holds us within our chilling grasp!
It binds the loving spirit in its persuasive paranoia:
that no one can be trusted,
everyone is corrupt,
nobody really cares about us.
Restore in our hearts the freedom of forgiveness,
the honest humility of love,
the ability to look beyond our rage to the day of
reconciliation — the healing restoration of broken
relationships and broken hearts.
O Lord, may this be our day of reconciliation!
Give us courage to release our rage,
to forget our pain,
to forgive our past.
Give us faith to see beyond
the logic of legalism
to the foolishness of forgiveness,
the freedom of love.
Set us free from our fear, we pray. Amen.

Prayers For Healing And Forgiveness (3)

O God of Grace, forgive our tendency to jump to
conclusions, to make false assumptions about people,
to judge others severely,
to categorize them permanently,
to ignore tham completely.
Give us the courage to remain open to the possibility
of change in people,
to keep looking for the movement of your Spirit in
their lives,
to keep hoping and thinking the best of others rather
than presuming the worst.
Lift our negative thoughts, our chronic cynicism,
our impetuous doubts out of the somber cells and bleak
hallways of our minds.
Show us that light of hope, that spark of faith that
will release the power of believing in justice,
goodness and human conversion.
If people do not change, we are all condemned!
Let us give to others the belief you have in us
and trust that love invites love,
                    forgiveness encourages forgiveness,
                    understanding increases understanding.
O God, grow in us a large heart. Amen.

Prayers For Healing And Forgiveness (4)

Author of our words of love,
Poet of our passions,
Composer of our dreams, we thank you for your Word
which supports us, inspires us and calls us out of
ourselves and into the world.
Help us, O Lord, to examine our words, to choose them
carefully. For we know that the tongue is, indeed,
a powerful instrument for blessing or curse.
Out of the same mouth can come words of healing and
hope or destruction and cruelty.
So eliminate from our hearts chronic diseases of
bitterness, hatred and anger that we may be free to
love abundantly, to grow in appreciation of differences
and to accept our own inadequacy in order to tolerate
and forgive the mistakes of others.
For we have all fallen short.
None of us seems able to aspire to the ideal of
ourselves, to grow up in the image of Christ, to reach
perfection.
Perhaps the most perfect thing we can do is admit
our own imperfection, confess our common humanity
and be as gentle in forgiving ourselves as Christ
is with us.
Then it may be possible for us to look with more
compassion upon others who have offended or wronged
us, perhaps even to forgive them.
O Lord, release us from the traps of superiority and
condemnation that our words may no longer be screams
of anger but shouts of "Alleluia!" Amen.

Prayers For Healing And Forgiveness (5)

The whisper of the night breeze and the light of the
morning remind us that you are near, O God.
When we feel like quitting and have no more strength
to go on,
when the effort of life becomes more difficult than
enjoyable,
when those we called "friend" betray a confidence
or refuse to understand our pain,
then, O God, our hearts groan and ache for your
presence.
Lighten the load of loneliness.
Revive our broken dreams;
heal our broken hearts;
restore our broken promises;
forgive our failure to keep commitments.
When life surrounds us like a dark shroud of death,
insult or pettiness, so that our very breath is taken
from us,
then come quickly, Lord, and breathe into us the
everlasting hope, the enduring dream, the permanent
promise of the Gospel.
Father of love, who commands us to live with faith,
compassion and justice, lift our cares from
self-serving preoccupations to stretch out into all
the world and reach the hungry, the abandoned, the
crushed, the sick, the dying — to people everywhere
who are just like us! Amen.

Prayers For Faith And Commitment (1)

Great and Mysterious God,
you come to us like the silent flight of the eagle,
as suddenly as a summer storm on the desert sands,
as imperceptibly as the wind charting the course of
large sailing ships.
Yet, because of our small faith, we cannot see you.
We look for you in giants; you show yourself in the
least of all.
We ask for demonstrations of great and wondrous feats;
you quietly and consistently send your soft, still
love in people we call friends and family — ordinary
people with plain histories and unassuming countenance.
We ask for rest from the toil and struggle of
our lives; you send us a person in need, a concern
for the politically oppressed, a care for the diseased
and dying, a heart for the poor and suffering.
You lead us to discover that true rest is found in
working for love,
peace is perceived in the out-pouring of forgiveness,
joy becomes real when compassion consumes our minds
and spirits.
Great God, you are with us when the sun warms our
bodies and when the storm strikes our lives.
May we be yours in rain and shine, in silence and
speech, in joy and sorrow, in rich times and poor,
for better or worse.
Make in our hearts a heavenly marriage of commitment
to your word and work. Amen.

Prayers For Faith And Commitment (2)

O Lord, you have called us to be your disciples and
to come to you even without credentials, complete
commitment or a full understanding of who you are
and what your commission requires of us.
You speak, and the words, "Follow me," stop us in
our tracks.
Everything is changed!
We question our goals and the direction of our lives.
That which seemed so clear and consumed so much of
our energy yesterday appears so senseless and vain
today.
Today, at the sound of your voice, at your invitation:
"Follow me!"
We stop our ears and run from your presence.
We flee from that power which we instinctively know
will change our lives.
You say, "Follow me," and pretense is exposed.
You say, "Follow me," and our collection of things
seems so silly.
You say, "Follow me," and our will to power fades
into a will to love.
How foolish you seem to us, O Lord, to call us to
discipleship; we are often unwilling, certainly
unworthy, seldom courageous, never without doubt.
Still, you seek us out, you bring us close, you take
us along with the simple invitation whispered to our
hearts:
"Come, and follow me!"
Yes, Lord, yes. Amen.

Prayers For Faith And Commitment (3)

Christ of the Upward Way,
blend your will into the fabric of our souls.
Mend our lives with the enduring thread of your love.
May our hearts grow larger.
May our minds receive new insight and greater wisdom.
May our wills find the nerve to accept your call to discipleship.
We have come to know the risk of living as though
love were possible for all people, as though
truth, if held too firmly, would one day prevail,
as though God cared about each of us in a special
way.
Such notions make us appear foolish in the wisdom
of this world.
Give us strength to keep this faith, to believe it
with our bodies as well as our minds, to share it
even in the most inopportune moments, when discretion
would dictate we remain silent.
For you are the Christ,
Giver of mercy;
You are the Lord,
Giver of life!
Beyond this truth there is none greater;
beyond this hope there is none higher.
Lift our spirits to believe once again that your caring
reaches deep into the hearts of all people
and brings us closer together as children of God.
Amen.

Prayers For Faith And Commitment (4)

Persistent and Long-Suffering God,
you have spoken your word to us, but we have not
listened. Your word has been planted in our hearts,
but we have not called upon it and expressed it in
our mouths.
We have learned how to love from your Son, our Lord,
Jesus Christ, yet what poor students we are!
How quickly we forget.
How easily we turn aside from those who are hurting,
those who are cast aside by the powerful in our
society, those who dwell in the darkness and solitude
of a prison or nursing home, those who walk the cold
streets shivering and hungry — never knowing from where
their next morsel of bread or warm drink will come.
Give us, O Lord, the eyes of faith that perceive the
pain and the heartache of the world and the will to
respond with a word of hope, an act of compassion.
Remind us that we have all been called to Christian
service, to discipleship, to evangelism — sharing the
"good news" of Christ's love by what we say and do
so that one day every knee will bow in gratitude and
joy for the presence of Jesus Christ in their lives.
Amen.

Prayers For Faith And Commitment (5)

Amazing God, Caring Father, your promise of hope
sustains and directs our lives.
We are not stopped by disappointments, nor thwarted
by disaster.
Life continues to spring from the ashes of death;
love persists in winning over separation;
the harvest sprouts above the barren fields;
the morning sun brightens the haunting blackness of
night.
Is this not the faith you have given us in your Spirit,
O God: to believe in the unbelievable,
       to see the invisible,
       to hope the impossible?
It is this faith which gives us courage to join others
in the pursuit of justice and equal rights for all.
It is this faith that affirms the worth of every human
being,
that carries the unpopular banners of righteousness
and judgment in a world morally soft and careless
in commitments,
that refuses to accept the way things are when they
can be made better.
We are thankful, O God, for the opportunities in this
life to share your grace and to participate in your
mission of healing and reconciliation.
May we wake each morning with your prayer on our lips
and your love in our hearts. Amen.

Prayers About Time And Work (1)

O God who is with us even in your darkest hour,
we thank you for this day and the days we have spent
in our counsel.
O Lord, our days on this earth are so short in number,
yet how we waste them!
When our days are rich with success and health, we
feel we do not need you.
And when our days are filled with tragedy and
heartache, we bitterly shut you out.
Open our minds and hearts to the joy and comfort of
your Son, Jesus Christ.
Melt our icebergs of pride and resentment;
transform our petty complaints into creative concerns.
Keep us from expecting too much of each other and
demanding too much from you.
Help us bear our disappointments, doubts and
frustrations with courage and grace, rather than
looking for someone to blame.
How difficult it is to take responsibility for our
own decisions, for our own situations, our own lives.
Yet, how else can we hope to change the ugliness of
the world?
Give us the strength of faith to confess our weaknesses
and to accept the mistakes of others.
Most of all, give us hope to keep on trying, go on
living and continue loving in the name of him whose
love never dies. Amen.

Prayers About Time And Work (2)

You have called, Lord, and we have heard the sound
of your voice.
Give us the courage of the early disciples to respond
with the same eagerness and expectation,
to leave our familiar ways and venture the way of
faith,
to trust that you would not ask from us what you have
not already provided.
We cast our nets upon the waters and come back empty-
handed.
We spend so much time working, yet our work seems
pointless, unsatisfying, burdensome.
Transform our work into worship,
our play into prayer,
our sorrow into singing.
Fill our time full of your Spirit.
Give us a glimpse of your Kingdom shining through
the gray mist of our confusion.
May we sense you near to us,
arm around our shoulders,
pointing out the signs and sounds of your Kingdom
on earth.
May we learn how to tell time not from our watches
but from your word,
not from our success but our faithfulness,
not by what we gain but what we give.
Make us fishers of the human heart and disciples of
your love. Amen.

Prayers About Time And Work (3)

O Creator of all our days, you have given us time
to live and time to discover the meaning of our lives.
May we make good use of the time you have given us
to experience and express the depth of our love.
May we embrace each day as a gift from the Holy Spirit,
something sacred and special:
a day designed for renewed resolve;
a day to overcome our fears and reach out to someone;
a day to stretch our faith by trying something new;
a day to play with children, visit an older person,
hug a friend;
a day to do something unexpected, something generous
and kind;
a day to reconcile a long-standing grudge, to forgive
and let it go.
Teach us to count how few our days that we may gain
wisdom of heart and appreciate the opportunities of
each day to grow closer to you and closer to each
other.
Help us, O Lord, to prepare for the best of life
so we will be prepared for the worst,
to glorify Christ and enjoy him
so we will be confident of his friendship in our time
of need.
May we dance in the sun with your Spirit
so we can find our way at midnight,
so we can walk through the darkness with the light
of life, even your Son, our Lord Jesus Christ! Amen.

Prayers About Time And Work (4)

O God of Life, we worship you not only with songs
of praise;
we worship you in our work, our daily toil, the labor
of our hearts.
We worship you in everything we say and do.
We pray that our worship may be acceptable in your
sight, that the effort we expend will not be in vain.
We pray that our work may provide life:
that someone's life will be made a little better,
that someone's pain will be eased,
that someone's load will be lighter.
So much of what we do seems so ordinary, O Lord.
Far from being a choir singing, "Hallelujahs,"
our work sounds like a snore in the pews!
Wake us to the movement of your Spirit.
May we not lose heart in the living of our lives.
Remind us that it is not so much what we do
but why we do it, for whom, in whose glory.
And help us remember it is also important how we work.
When we work with joy and exuberance,
when we work faithfully and reliably,
when we work with honesty and integrity,
when we work cooperatively and with care,
then, O Lord, we work for you and through the leading
of your Spirit.
Bless our work and our worship, we pray. Amen.

Prayers About Time And Work (5)

O Lord, you have made this day and called it good.
You have provided us with everything we need to make
it glorious.
Your tree of life is in full blossom, abundant with
the fruit for physical and spiritual nourishment.
But we sit under its shadow and wonder what to do!
We stand in the darkness without realizing we are
shaded from your dazzling light.
We sample the harvest of our hard work and forget
to be thankful for the generous return of our labors.
We forget there are others who work harder and get
back less.
And there are others who have stopped working because
of fatigue and a sense of futility.
O God, give us the heart that stretches into all the
world and takes the hands of brothers and sisters
who hunger and thirst in body, mind and spirit for
the hope which can only come to us through Christ's
saving love.
Help us to reach deep into our own hearts as we reach
out to others and share with them the daily bread
you offer to us so generously.
May we hear the knock on the door.
May we see the beggar on the street.
May we sense the need of those who cry themselves
to sleep each night from the pain of hunger.
May your bread which is broken
be shared with all the world. Amen.

Prayers For The Journey (1)

Like dormant seeds in winter soil, we wait for your
sunshine and your rain to nourish us, to call us out
of the ground and into the light of day with the new
hope that comes from your radiant Son, Jesus Christ.
O Lord and Creator, sustainer of our lives,
we praise you for giving us some revelation of who
you are so we might know who we are.
For your mystery penetrates our very soul.
We participate in the wonder of your creation,
never fully grasping its depth and origin,
and yet trusting in its progress and its advance into
the future because we trust the cultivator of this
garden of life.
You are the Gardener, the one who watches over every
flower, every blossom, every plant, every seed.
And so, O God, instill within us that faith which
trusts what it does not know, that vision which sees
what eyes cannot penetrate, that heart which responds
and pulsates to the one who calls it home.
Help us, O Lord, to trust the journey of life,
to believe in your leading,
to seek your guidance,
to appreciate your will,
to follow you with obedience and joy so we may become
that which we have been called to be,
your very own.
We pray in the name of him who taught us to love,
taught us to learn from life and to never stop
learning,
to ask questions that go beyond answers
and to follow our faith wherever it leads. Amen.

Prayers For the Journey (2)

Loving God, there are so many paths that beckon our
following,
so many destinies that summon our allegiance.
And yet, we know that beyond any roles we play in
life — father or mother, husband or wife, child or
teenager, grandparent, business person — there is only
one calling,
to be a disciple of Jesus Christ.
Give us that courage which enables us to live within
your grace, to strive to become all you want us to
become,
to speak the truth as we have learned it from your
word,
to be present with those who are forgotten by society,
to stand with the powerless and the weak,
to risk being unpopular and out of step with everyone
else in order to walk in your way.
O God, our lives are filled with such vagaries and
such ambiguity.
It is difficult to sort it out and to know what is
right and what is wrong.
Help us learn to trust
that when we seriously intend your will and prayerfully
seek it each day, we will sense the direction and
presence of your Spirit.
Be with us, O God, as we seek to be yours and to follow
your way.
Amen.

Prayers For The Journey (3)

We have wandered away, but you come and search for
us, O God.
We feel lost and confused, but you would have us be
found and shown the way.
Do not forget us, O God, even when we have forgotten
you.
Do not depart from us even when we turn our faces
from your side.
Direct us with your gentle touch, your still, small
voice which speaks to our hearts and minds, urging
us back to that which is sensible, spiritual — that
straight, sure road that leads to the abundant life.
From the dark rooms of despair and depression, sadness,
guilt and grief, save us, O Lord.
Become our door to life, to the blazing light that
stirs our spirits and gives us good hope.
In our walled rooms of cynicism, where we hang pictures
of life, open a window to the wonder of the real life
you set before us — a life of infinite possibilities,
eternal purpose.
Breathe your Spirit into us, O God, that we may sense
the inspiration of your love and have confidence in
your guidance.
Amen.

Prayers For The Journey (4)

God of Grace, forgive our failure to live up to our
faith.

Bridge the chasm that separates what we believe from
what we do.

Teach us to be more consistent in value and virtue.

Make us aware of our hypocrisy, self-righteousness,
arrogance and self-deceit.

Lead us away from temptation to the triumph over our
passions and preoccupations.

Lead us out of the darkness of doubt and guilt into
the light of faith and forgiveness.

Lead us up from the valley of sorrow and grief to
the hills of hope and joy.

Lead us away from the noisy, chattering crowds to
the spiritually-rich silence of solitude.

And lead us out of our loneliness to the caring
community which you have called together to confess
sin,

to forgive one another,

to love as you have taught us to love,

and to pray as you have taught us to pray. Amen.

Prayers For The Journey (5)

Teach us your ways, O Lord, that we may run and not
grow weary, walk and not faint.
Take our hand and lead us to your path of
righteousness.
Guide us through the storm of grief and fear.
Take us through troubled times.
Walk with us through our worries and heartaches.
Spread your highway of hope through our hearts that
we too may become the way of life.
O Lord, following you, may we become a pathway of
peace for those troubled by tragedy or threat;
may we provide the way of liberating love, bringing
release to the captive — prisoners of conscience or
prisoners of psychological oppression and guilt;
may we be your way of loving acceptance that lifts
the heart that is alone and brings hope to dark
despair.
Teach us your way, O Lord. Amen.

Prayers For The Journey (6)

O Lord, open our eyes to the work of your Spirit.
Remind us that we are not alone in the living of our
days but that we are coaxed by your Spirit, counseled
by your Son.
Thank you, Father, for opening new doors to us
when the familiar passage ways become blocked and
closed.
Thank you for keeping us from the dead-end streets
of life and showing us the path to your highway of
hope.
Help us to trust that you lead us in the paths of
righteousness for your name's sake.
And even though we walk through the shadows of
darkness,
your inner light shows us the way to lasting hope,
peace that passes understanding, inconceivable joy.
May we allow your Spirit to work in our hearts,
to whisper to our will,
to inflame our desire,
to widen our vision
so that we may not only repeat your prayer but believe
its timeless message. Amen.

Prayers For The Journey (7)

O God of Hope, you sent John the Baptizer to prepare
us for the arrival of your Son.
But still we are not ready!
We have grown away from you and so think we have grown
up.
We are comfortable leading our lives out of
self-interest and would find self-sacrifice an
unwelcome intruder.
We believe it is better to help ourselves than to
help others;
better to not "bother" our neighbor than to be his
brother;
better to avoid those who differ from us than to
appreciate their mystery;
better to compete and overpower than to cooperate
and reconcile.
But you aren't listening!
You continue to send those who remind us to make ready.
You send them in the form of
the powerless victims of India who breathe the deadly
air of commercial ambition and neglect,
the bloated bellies of black Africans who slowly die
for lack of bread,
the shivering stranger on the streets of our cities
who stands alone, homeless and hopeless.
You send them in the least of these among us whose
gaunt and gray faces cry out: "Prepare the way of
the Lord!"
Come quickly Jesus into our hearts and minds that
we may become the hands of your healing, the heralds
of your hope. Amen.

Prayers For The Journey (8)

O Lord, Our God, travel with us through the turmoil
of our lives.
When death, divorce or disaster must be faced
grant us your strength.
We know the rain falls on the just and the unjust.
Our only hope is the promise of your sun!
We look for the light of a new day.
We wait for a breath of fresh air.
We work for the coming of your Kingdom.
For those who struggle over the wages of war and seek
the sanity of peaceful resolve,
grant them your peace.
For those who fight loneliness and despair and need
the encouragement of a good friend,
grant them your love.
For those who lie sick in bed, torn in body or troubled
in mind,
grant them your healing.
For those who are still outraged over human suffering,
oppressive social structures or casual consciences,
grant them courage to speak their convictions.
Let the voice of pain and prophecy be heard in this
land that the God of mercy and majesty may demonstrate
his creative power.
We are not lost, for you are the Lord of our lives.
You find us in our hiding places and bid us to follow
you to the way of truth and life. Amen.

Prayers For The Journey (9)

On the dark side of the soul, we wander aimlessly,
hopelessly, lost in our spiraling fears, our deep
sorrows.
We look for a dream to chase away the nightmares,
a shaft of light to pierce the darkness.
And then you come to us . . . unannounced, unexpected.
You come to us in the confidence that people we admire
place in us.
You appear in the fellowship of forgiveness and
healing.
You speak to us through words that affirm, encourage,
build up and empower.
You follow us into empty spaces, then gently lead
us back to firm foundations.
Continue, O Lord, to search us out and call us from
our hiding places.
Give us strength to resist being swallowed up in grief,
frozen by loneliness, destroyed by loss or failure.
Help us to find the sweet communion of kindred souls
who dare to reveal their wounds and so convey their
courage and comfort.
Remind us that the way of love is complicated,
difficult and fraught with pain, yet it is the only
way worth following, the only truth worth believing,
the only life worth living.
Grant us faith to live it and to look for it. Amen.

Prayers For The Journey (10)

O God of Purity and Peace, you have given us many
visions of holiness.
We have heard from your prophets and from our Lord
Jesus Christ how abundant and beautiful life becomes
when lived under your care and direction.
Still, we seek our own paths, our own way.
We wander down rugged, twisted roads cluttered with
the debris of destructive decisions.
Lead us back to the straight and narrow path of
discipleship and decency.
Lead us back to self-respect by filling our hearts
with self-giving love.
May we seek to serve others instead of satisfying
our every desire.
And may our greatest desire, our most powerful passion
be to see the coming of your Kingdom on earth and
the love of Christ in every heart.
Forgive us for falling short and help us to grow long
in love and humility. Amen.

All Seasons (1)

Tender and Merciful Father,
the seasons of our lives are ever-changing and
continually unfold your subtle truths.
The autumn colors of red and brown are transformed
by the sudden fall of pristine flakes of ice.
Winter is introduced by the flapping wings of the
mysterious migratory flight of your feathered creatures
of grace.
The resurrection of hope is played out in the pageantry
of spring, the push of dormant flowers out of the
dark earth into the bright, dancing rays of sunlight.
Over and over again, year after year,
we are reminded of your promise of life,
the power of growth and change.
The eastern light daily climbing above the dark
mountains testifies to the reliability of your word.
Give us faith to rise above the plateau of contentment
to the mountainous heights you have planned for us,
to the loneliness that drives us toward deep
friendships,
to the fears that push us to risks of courage,
to the doubts that force us to broaden our faith,
and to the humility of facing our own mistakes in
order to forgive the mistakes of others.
Christ of our conscience and compassion, become the
center of our lives and our reason for love. Amen.

All Seasons (2)

Like a gray quilted comforter, your clouds drape over
our city, O God.
While we speak of "bad weather,"
you prepare to nourish the grass and flowers with
your rain.
We sense a coziness, a closeness to you on days like
this.
The vast universe and infinite space are reduced to
a soft ceiling of fluffy clouds.
How carefully you have planned your creation, O Lord.
You knew that our minds would need occasional relief
from the contemplation of immense sky and dense stars,
that there would be times when the courage it takes
to live would need sheltering and renewal.
So like a giant womb your dark clouds encompass us
and render a sense of comfort,
a pause from the frenzied activity of life,
an offer of a change of plans.
We are grateful Father for the variety and richness
of nature and the changing seasons of our lives:
for the season of childlike abandon and bouncing
energy;
for the season of teenage romance and idealism;
for the season of young determination to change the
world and make it better;
for the season of regeneration, of leading children
to your Spirit;
and for the season of wisdom, reflection and simple
gratitude for the length of our days.
O Lord, we are thankful for all our days and for that
Spirit which supports us daily. Amen.

All Seasons (3)

In the midst of our interminable distractions and
busy lives, you confront us with your love,
O God of Grace.
And we are forced to struggle with the reality of
a power quite beyond our own:
a power that supports us through times of sickness
and suffering;
a power that stimulates creativity and courage to
explore new options;
a power that quiets our fears and renews our faith
in the future;
a power that lifts our hearts with joy and hope
even from the deepest disappointment and sorrow.
For you are the Christ, giver of mercy;
you are the Lord, giver of grace.
You were with us in the innocence of our youth as
we danced and played and were unaware of your watching;
you were with us in the turmoil of our teens when
we were sorting out our dreams;
you were with us at those peak points of joy when
love is conceived and new birth enters our lives,
and our hearts.
And you are there in the valleys of our lives when
we feel defeated, lost or alone.
O God, who is with us even when we desert you,
have mercy on us and keep us in your tender care.
Amen.

All Seasons (4)

O God of ancient pioneer, distant traveler, transient
stranger, we need direction for our lives.
We are pilgrims on this planet traveling through space
with the limited timetable you gave to each of us.
May we use time
and not kill it,
fulfill time
and not cut it short.
May we always be aware of the sacred gift of life
and strive to spend it wisely.
Direct us, O Lord, with the morning star into a new
day.
Guide us by the freedom of the wind that tosses the
trees and soothes the grass.
Deliver us from the drought and lethargy of life into
a gentle rainfall which waters our hidden seed and
brings forth fruit.
Lead us through paths of darkness so we may appreciate
the splendor of your brilliant light.
Lure us from loneliness to the risk of love.
Save us from complacency by placing before us a
challenging opportunity, a disturbing thought, an
irresistible option.
Wean us from the dependency of infancy;
liberate us from the anxiety of adolescence;
pull us beyond the fires of our first love;
and prepare us for the burden and exhilaration of
adulthood.
Prime our hope and courage as we face life's declining
years and walk before us through the door of death
so we may follow with peaceful dignity.
O God of destiny, chart the course of lives and
give us faith to see the way and follow the footsteps
of our Lord. Amen.

All Seasons (5)

O God of Life, you come to us in the spring of our
faith when we learn for the first time the meaning
of your love,
when the sparkle and thrill of a fresh insight, a
worthy challenge or a courageous cause excites our
minds and our hearts.
And you stay with us through the summer of our faith,
when we grow in wisdom and understanding, compassion
and nerve,
when we feel the warmth of your abiding presence,
the heat of your truth.
We know you are present in the autumn of our faith,
when the winds of time and experiences of life tease
away the dead leaves of our doctrine:
assumptions that have not held true,
naive beliefs that have held on to petty prejudice
and fearful doubts that must be driven away.
But we are most grateful that you do not fail us in
the winter of our faith,
when death is at our door
or loss of loved ones becomes almost commonplace.
For we continue to hope and look for the day of new
growth,
when life completes its cycle,
when things that die give rise to new birth, new life,
new faith in your everlasting mercy,
in your constant companionship
and in your Son, our Redeemer. Amen.

Autumn (1)

Great God of autumn splendor, flashing color and
howling winds, we stand in awe at the power and majesty
of your creation.
It makes us wonder how such a great and mighty God,
creator of all humankind, could care personally for
each of us!
How grateful we are to worship a loving Father who
makes himself accessible to our prayers, the ache
in our hearts, the dreams in our minds, the yearning
in our souls.
Hear our prayers, O Lord!
Hear the pure prayer of the child spoken with unguarded
honesty.
Hear the painful prayer of the sick and dying that
testifies to your suffering love and constant concern.
Hear the lonely prayer of the imprisoned,
the shut-in, the hostage, the very old.
Hear the doubting prayer of the worrier, the defeated,
the depressed.
Hear the angry prayer of the victims of injustice,
the unemployed, the crime victims, the handicapped.
Hear, O Lord, the grateful prayers of those who have
found themselves, discovered new life, embraced new
hope, discarded an ugly habit or heard your answer.
And hear the prayer without words that is spoken in
silence by those who keep the faith, help the weak,
strengthen the faint-hearted and strive for peace.
O hear the prayer of all your children who you taught
to pray together. Amen.

Autumn (2)

Creator God, we praise you for the wonders of this
world, the seasons of the year and the seasons of
our lives.
With autumn's coat of many colors we are reminded
you created your children to be a beautiful bouquet
of color and custom which, when gathered together,
adorns the table of the Lord.
Winter's unbiquitous white blanket of soft snow
transforms the ugly scars of carved-out countryside
— our trash and ashes —
into a wonderland of radiance and artistic form.
In the same way, your forgiving grace wipes away the
ugly scars of our past and makes us whiter than snow.
The resurrection of life in the spring is a profound
testimony to the power of your Spirit which recreates
hope in the midst of despair and restores joy to a
broken heart.
The warm summer days invite us out to play,
to dance in the meadow and sing praises to God,
the one who is with us through all of life's changes.
Give us faith to trust the changes,
to look for the new creation you fashion in our hearts
and in our lives,
even as we trust in your love which never changes.
Amen.

New Years And Tomorrow (1)

God of New Years, new hopes and new promises,
lead us into the future with faith and a sense of
purpose.
May our lives not be haphazard, but committed and
deliberate.
Out of the wreckage of too many failures,
too many hurts,
too much hesitation,
too little courage and too few victories,
restore our confidence and faith in the power of your
presence.
This Body of Christ is not without blemish and bruises;
it may suffer from fatigue and shortness of breath;
but it believes in your new life.
May we dream dreams and dare to try new ways of sharing
your love.
As we close the door of one year and open our windows
to a new year, give us the strength of heart and
clarity of mind to see what needs to be done
and do it;
to hear the sound of loneliness
and fill it with compassion;
to take the hand of children
and lead them into your kingdom;
to heal the sick of body and mind,
and care for the isolated and lost.
May the wisdom of the old, which comes from long,
alert experience, and the idealism and energy of youth,
produce new insight and creativity in your church
and in the world.
How happy we are to know that you are our God,
and that neither death, nor life, nor the events of
the past, nor the fear of the future can keep us from
everlasting grace.
Spirit of Scripture, be with us in the birth, death
and resurrection of Jesus Christ, we pray. Amen.

New Years And Tomorrow (2)

God of Grace, forgive our distractions, our
preoccupations, our areas of self-interest, our doubts
and fears — whatever keeps us from thanksgiving, from
the joy of Christian service, from an unswerving faith
in your promises of life, love and laughter.
We are distraught by threats of economic disaster,
skyrocketing inflation, mass starvation, homeless
refugees, nuclear mismanagement and political turmoil
which plague this planet.
As we look ahead we perceive a future that at best
looks dismal. But we are called to a perverted faith
which goes against the common stream, which resists
despair.
We are people of an obstinate faith which stands in
a tradition of the impossible becoming real.
We are children of faith
whose bright hope looks almost innocently to the future
in realizing our limitations and discovering our final
dependency on your guidance and strength.
O God, who believes in us, may we never cease to
believe in you
even when disappointment and crisis destroy the comfort
and security of our family life.
For you have given us the gift of a higher hope that
can look over doom and see the dawning of a new day,
that transcends our daily plight as we let ourselves
become part of a larger effort, a greater cause, a
holy existence.
We believe, O God, help our unbelief!
Give us courage for the living of these days. Amen.

New Years And Tomorrow (3)

O God of yesterday, today and tomorrow, reassure our
hearts and minds that you are very present with us
everyday of our lives,
that the distance we experience comes from our own
faltering faith and not from a withdrawal of your
love and concern.
For you catch every tear and know every heartbeat
of compassion.
We worry about tomorrow
but you would have us focus on the needs of today.
We worry about international conflict and where it
is headed;
you would remind us of our conflict of loyalty that
leads to problems in our family, among friends and
in our community.
We wonder when the world will come to an end;
you invite us to end preoccupation with
self-gratification, greed and pride.
Give us a new heart to feel beyond our own tiny circle
of family and friends the pain and suffering of people
who are strangers to us — people in unknown lands or
the unknown neighbor next door.
Fill our heads with your wisdom, O God,
with that truth which sees beyond contentment with
status quo to the inequities and unfairness that exist
therein.
Give us a shock of righteous indignation when any
suffer or go hungry or are oppressed or are unfairly
treated.
And grant us a mouth to speak boldly and with
confidence your word of hope.
May your word come to us spontaneously and filled
with light and love as we look to you in trust. Amen.

Spring (1)

O God, our Father, the fresh signs of life in our
gardens and lawns tell us it is spring.
The sound of flapping wings against the blue sky
reminds us of that migratory urge that calls us to
adventure, that arouses our dulled senses to the
excitement of a new day.
The green buds of this season strengthen our faith
in the universal persistence of life.
That which has died now has produced a veritable array
of color, shape and texture.
Hope which has laid dormant under the heavy ground
of sadness, grief and loneliness is beginning to stir
and make its way to the sun.
O Lord of life, who showers us with his love so our
hands will become like honey to sweeten the world
with their touch,
help us to hear the music of spring,
the symphony of friendship,
the harmonious chorus of the community of believers.
Give us courage to face the hard trials that would
make us grow and to find peace in decisions fashioned
by prayer and compassion.
Come quickly, Lord, and find a place in our homes
where hope abounds and laughter flows freely.
Amen.

Spring (2)

O Great Creator God,
we are thankful for all the days of our lives,
but we are especially grateful for days of dancing
sunshine and seasons of growth,
when tender green shoots raise their bulbous heads
above the winter's barren ground,
when a chorus of birds convene in the trees for a
family reunion from their days of southern migration.
We thank you, O God, for the hope that returns to
our hearts when we can walk outside bathed in warmth
and beauty.
We pray for all who are still enduring the winter
of their lives:
the cold chill of grief,
the cool breeze of loneliness,
the icy shiver of broken relationships, broken dreams,
broken hearts.
May they continue to look for the spring,
to await the return of blue skies and bright smiles,
the comfort of a close friend,
the assurance of constant prayer.
For you are our springtime God who restores new life;
but you are also with us in winter, sharing your
blanket of dreams.
And so we hope in him who knows cold and heat,
darkness and light,
despair and courage
and teaches us a springtime prayer. Amen.

Spring (3)

With the softness of spring-falling snow,
your love falls down upon us, O Lord.
We are touched by a new sensation,
a growing awareness of your gentle activity in our
lives.
Continue, O Lord, to open our eyes to the miracles
your love has fashioned:
the miracle of music that reaches our minds through
tiny membranes and bone fragments;
the miracle of healing in simple expressions like . . .
I'm sorry
I'll stay with you
It's okay
You're going to make it
I care for you
Let me be your friend.
There is the miracle of the persistent order of things
affirmed with each sunrise and sunset.
And the wonders of new birth . . .
a baby
a graduate
a bride and groom
a new insight
a profound experience
laughter after many tears
a morning sunbeam across the dark walls of fear.
Make us your miracle workers of love, O God of Grace.
Teach us the power of compassion, acceptance,
friendliness, forgiveness.
In our wonder of your great sacrifice of love,
give us the will to follow.
May your prayer be evidenced in our lives even as
it is spoken from our lips. Amen.

Prayers About Suffering, Dying And Grief (1)

O Saving Lord, you invited us to your table
and we came gladly, quickly, eagerly.
We ate of your bread and it was good.
But now you call us to the cross
and we halt along the path, stand frozen along the
way.
We fall to our knees,
great drops of sweat bead on our foreheads as fear
absorbs our faith.
Our bodies tremble in anguish.
O Lord, we gave you our minds.
We offered you our disciplined devotion.
We loved you with our whole heart.
Must you have our bodies as well?
Can we hold on to nothing?
Must everything be given to you?
O Lord, if it be possible, let this cup pass from
us.
Let us somehow avoid the pain, the suffering, the
physical agony of life.
We would weep over others.
We would pray continually for others.
But let your cup of pain pass our lips.
O Lord, may we embrace a faith that goes
beyond our experience,
beyond sight and sound,
beyond trembling nerve
and affirm, nevertheless, you are our Redeemer.
May we trust not only our minds and spirits
but our bodies as well.
Give us faith to walk with you,
not only to the upper room,
but to Golgotha
keeping our eyes ever up the hill of grace.
For you have promised that we will never walk alone
but that you walk with us
even as you have walked before us.
In the name of our loving Lord Jesus Christ, we pray.
Amen.

Prayers About Suffering, Dying And Grief (2)

When life is too much for us to bear
and we feel life is against us,
then where, O God, can we turn?
To whom can we look for relief?
You, O Lord, are our ever present help in times of
trouble and heartache.
For you are the God who was broken
that we may be mended.
You are the God who was crucified
in order for the powers of darkness to be destroyed.
O God of Love,
may we not forget you.
Help us to remember you in our suffering.
For in remembering your grief,
we know we have a friend in our sorrows;
in remembering your death,
we know we are not alone in our dying;
in remembering your resurrection,
we know that you can create victory out of disaster.
Let not the consuming concerns of the present
overshadow the promise of past joy and future hope.
As people of his story,
may we not forget the Author of Life,
the one who writes the last word — the word of love
eternal,
love inseparable,
love that prays in and through us. Amen.

Prayers About Suffering, Dying And Grief (3)

Hear, O Lord, the prayers of love's loss;
we who are numbed by the shock of recent tragedy or
death.
May the cry of anguish which echoes through the hollow
of our hearts be heard by your alert Spirit.
When the bolts of pain tear our life in two,
when our grief wells inside us to overflowing,
when fear steals our breath and robs our courage,
when the struggle for hope is defeated by the
announcement, "It's over,"
then, Great God, catch our crumbling bodies and sinking
spirits and gently soothe our crinkled brows, our
trembling souls.
Draw near to us,
stand with us
and let your silence absorb our tears and screams.
Listen to our ranting and indignation.
Accept our raging sorrow, until at last
the storm is over and we collapse in your waiting
arms.
Then, O Lord, hold us close until your warmth returns
to our frozen season of sadness
and hope flows back into our hearts
and our eyes can once again focus on the beauty and
promise of your creation.
O crucified God,
we place our trust in your hands,
those scarred hands which have felt our pain and known
our sorrow,
the hands that cup ours in prayer. Amen.

Prayers About Suffering, Dying And Grief (4)

O Lord, you have prepared a place for us at your table
where we can discover nourishment and fellowship —
the bread of life,
the hands of friends.
There is a place in your house
where we can gather and worship,
where we can comfort those who are wounded
and celebrate those who have found new life in your
love.
There is a place in this world
where work becomes sacred,
where we offer to you our time and energy, our talent
and compassion, our faithfulness and courage.
And there is a place in your heart
that you have prepared for each of us —
a place that remains empty unless we come to you and
abide with you.
It is the same emptiness we experience
when our hearts are troubled and heavy-laden,
when the love we expressed through another seems to
die with them.
Give us good faith, O Lord, to perceive beyond our
pain that love which never dies,
that place in your heart which remains forever open,
that home in your house where we can find peace and
comfort.
And show us the empty places in this world you would
have us fill with your love — places where people are
sick and dying,
places where people sit behind bars
or thick storm windows
watching their lives pass by,
places where people search for food to fill the
emptiness inside.
Give us courage to go to these places,
wherever Christ leads,
so that together we can create a place of hope and
prayer. Amen.

Prayers About Suffering, Dying And Grief (5)

O faithful God of an unfaithful generation,
hear our cries of desperation, of grief, of pain.
We are hurting, Lord, and need a friend.
We suffer alone because we are afraid of driving off
our friends, of scaring them away.
So we smile bravely, but our glistening eyes give us
away.
We put up a courageous front while our foundation
crumbles.
We sit alone in homes for the aged staring out the
window looking for someone, waiting for something
to happen,
waiting to die.
We sit alone in steel-gray cells visited only by our
shame, our guilt, our self-hatred.
Or we crouch in cages for prisoners of conscience
because we spoke out against the powers of persecution
and torture.
We lie dying on beds of disease surrounded by tubes
and monitors, avoided by healers who hate to accept
defeat.
Be our friend, Lord. Come to us in the dark night
of sorrow and suffering and take our hands, whisper
a word of love, kiss our trembling cheeks.
Come to us, O Lord, in those who have learned
compassion and the meaning of your prayer. Amen.

Prayers About Suffering, Dying And Grief (6)

(Psalm 23)

The path of life becomes twisted and overgrown
with wild grass.
Show us the way, Good Shepherd.
We so easily become lost in blind canyons or
wander through dark woods.
Seek us out, Good Shepherd, and lead us to the paths
of righteousness.
When our lives become chaotic and conflicted,
tossed and torn by inner turmoil,
return us to calm, still waters,
to green pastures of peace and hope.
When our spirits are starving for the bread of life,
feed your sheep, Good Shepherd.
Restore our souls.
And when disease or death take us through dark valleys
shadowed with doubt and fear,
walk with us, Lord.
Lift us when we fall. Carry us when we can walk no
more, when our courage is exhausted, our faith spent.
Until at last we reach the other side —
the hills of hope, the mountain top of joy.
Then, with cups overflowing,
we will celebrate the feast of faith and
dwell in the house of the Lord forever. Amen.

Prayers About Suffering, Dying And Grief (7)

Beyond the veil of darkness,
beyond the shadow of doubt,
your love, O Lord, brings hope to our hearts.
It is this love that sustains us, this love that
keeps us alive,
gives us a reason for being,
tells us a truth beyond words.
For there are times, O Lord, when the valley of death
seems, oh, so deep,
when the future is blurred and bleak,
when our aloneness surrounds us like a low-flying cloud and
our blood runs cold with fear.

But the Man on the Tree
who was hung there for me
enters into my suffering,
makes a home in my hopelessness and
answers all my questions, "Why?"
with the same reply:
"Because I love you."

This love is enough, O Loving God.
May we believe it.
May we hold fast to it when all else fades,
when our lives turn sour,
when pain shatters our senses
and friends turn from us in their terror and
helplessness.
For it is the love you promised us from the
Suffering One, the one who taught us to keep on praying
through the pain. Amen.

Prayers About Suffering, Dying And Grief (8)

O Suffering God,
you have heard the groaning of this generation and
watched with sadness the heartbreaking history of
human destruction.
How great must be the burden you carry for your
children, O Parent God!
Still, you do not turn your face from us.
You have not separated yourself from us.
Your love and forgiveness remain through
our barrage of bitterness,
our raging ridicule,
our cry of anguish.
Again and again you approach us with tenderness,
patiently listening to our protests, our indignation,
our outrage.
The tears of human history could flood the world
but you gather them up and save them to sprinkle on
our heads at baptism.
Help us to remember that salvation comes through
suffering,
the suffering that is felt from facing honestly the
realities of this world:
the power of sin and selfishness;
our alienation from your will and way;
our jealousy of your power and our arrogant attempts
to exceed you at our altars of self-worship;
the fragmented result of living without your direction.
Have mercy on us, O Father!
Save us from ourselves and lead us by the light of
your Son. Amen.

Prayers About Suffering, Dying And Grief (9)

Everlasting God, Maker of Heaven and Earth,
our prayer looks up to you.
We watch the heavens for answers and hope the stars
will guide us,
but the night is still and the stars are distant.
We need a God who roars like a lion,
who makes his presence known to us,
who cares for us, each one, as though we were his
own,
who overlooks our foolish ways, our thoughtless remarks
and loves us despite ourselves.
Are you such a God?
Is this the meaning of that eternally unique human
encounter that led to the death of the one they called
the Christ?
Was he given new life so that we may know you will
not desert us,
not when we sorrow,
not when we grieve,
not when we suffer,
not even when we die?
Is this why he said he came to set us free:
so we may have life and live it more abundantly?
Such is a God beyond thought and comprehension!
Someone to be perceived only in the deepest region
of our hearts.
Something to be grasped only by our greatest dreams,
our fondest hopes, our dearest desires.
Let us believe you are our God, our Father, our Creator
and our Friend. Amen.

Prayers About Suffering, Dying And Grief (10)

(Memorial Day Prayer)

O God of Grace, we bring our heavy and sad hearts
to you as we remember those who have fought and died
for freedom,
those who have defied the powers and principalities
that seek to destroy your love and bury our faith,
those who made the ultimate sacrifice of giving up
their lives for their friends.
We also remember all those who, having lived this
life with faith, imparted your love, forgave their
offenders, shared their food with the hungry, clothed
the naked, educated the powerless, healed the sick,
strengthened the fainthearted,
now live eternally with you.
We miss them, O Lord.
They brought happiness, healing and hope into our
lives.
Laughter was not a stranger in their homes,
nor was there a lack of kindness and honesty.
We remember these, O Lord, and pray that we may also
be remembered for the days of our lives that were
lived in your will and that followed your way.
And we hope our days of darkness will be forgotten,
our sins forgiven, our pettiness and thoughtlessness
overlooked.
O Lord, if you never forgot our sins
who would be blameless?
How thankful we are for your great mercy!
We praise you that our lives are lived in your grace
and our hearts are free from the drab darkness of
guilt.
How blessed are we to worship a God who calls each
of us his child! Amen.

Prayers About Suffering, Dying And Grief (11)

O Great God of mercy and compassion,
visit your Spirit on those who suffer.
May those who seek constantly food enough for their
family be given daily bread.
May those who struggle with each waking moment the
pain and anguish of a diseased, crippled or wounded
body find relief and comfort.
May those who are facing surgery be assured of healing
and recovery.
May those who stand by helplessly watching and waiting
while those they love suffer or die be strengthened
by your Spirit.
For you are the God who became flesh in order to know
immediately our pain, to feel our wounds, to experience
our fear of death.
And you are the Father who wept over the world while
his Son was battered, bruised and left hanging to
die.
So you know us.
You suffer with us.
You care about our anguish.
And your love endures all things,
bears all things,
believes all things
and hopes all things.
In this love we find faith and courage to live and
breathe and have our being.
Thanks be to you, O God, for your love! Amen.

Prayers About Suffering, Dying And Grief (12)

Compassionate, cross-bearing God, you know the secret
places of the soul.
For you have borne our flesh and know our pain and
anguish:
the struggle of this life,
the feeling of helplessness,
the rage of righteous anger,
the tears of sorrow,
the loneliness of rejection and abandonment.
You have borne our sin and know how it burdens our
lives, how heavily it weighs on our broken hearts,
how it crushes our spirit and hope.
You have suffered with us and for us and know our
suffering.
You dry away our tears and comfort our quaking hearts.
Grant us the yoke of your love,
the cross of compassion,
the wings of faith.
Give us the heart of a servant,
the faith of a disciple
and the will to follow the sacrificial way of our
Lord Jesus Christ. Amen.

Prayers About Suffering, Dying And Grief (13)

O God of Hope and Joy,
how grateful are we that the hollow echo of the
funeral drum is not the last sound our spirits hear,
but rather the chorus of joyous angels singing your
"Alleluia!"
For Death, where is thy sting?
O Death, where is thy victory?
We celebrate the good news of death being swallowed
up in Christ's sacrifice on the cross.
There is no tragedy great enough to overcome the power
of hope you plant in our hearts, O God.
You mock the fears that master our minds.
You laugh at the evil that threatens to undo us.
You uncover the mask of malevolence and reveal your
benevolent Spirit.
Continue to surprise us with your miraculous power
of making all things new!
Startle us with the strange, unexpected ways you choose
to convey your gifts of love.
Prod us out of our cynical complacency to rejoice
in the victory of comedy over tragedy,
compassion over alienation,
Christ over suffering.
Help us to hear the promises you have spoken and to
believe. Amen.

Prayers About Suffering, Dying And Grief (14)

O God of Hope,
when one so close to us dies
death looms large within us.
It seems bigger than life.
It closes in on us.
It threatens to destroy our last thread of faith.
Was it a darkness like this you entered with your
light?
Was it a death like this from which you brought forth
life?
Is it the fear of separation from all that is vital,
joyful, lovely
that you answered with the firm assurance of your
inseparable love?
Thank you, dear God, for our resurrection faith,
our relationship with Jesus Christ,
our courage which comes from your Holy Spirit.
Comfort us, O Lord, we pray. Amen.

Prayers About Suffering, Dying And Grief (15)

(Death of a Child)

Loving Father, you stand next to us
when we need you most.
In this hour of sorrow, we turn to you
knowing that you stay with us,
knowing that you love us.
For there is not a joy which comes to us
nor a child who leaves us
that you are not present in the coming and going.
We praise you for the gift of this child,
for her (his) baptism into your church,
for the lives she (he) touched
and for the hearts that grew closer together in the
precious moments she (he) was with us.
We are grateful for the new life you have given her
(him) and the place you have saved for her (him)
close to your heart.
Now lift heavy hearts and give us good hope in your
promise of life eternal,
the comfort which comes from your Holy Spirit
and the faith in Jesus Christ our Lord,
who was dead but now lives eternally with you.
Amen.

As We Gather (1)

O God of Love, we dare to gather in your name because
we believe we are children of God.
Your love has somehow reached our hearts and touched
our lives.
Your truth has brightened our path and shown us the
way.
Your forgiveness has lightened the heavy load of life's
disappointments, tragedies and sorrow.
We come with the hope that you hear every prayer and
know our every hurt.
We believe you answer us with your persistent presence,
your unfaltering encouragement and your power of
endurance.
For we are people who are no strangers to suffering.
We have absorbed the arbitrary attack of crippling
disease or horrible accident in our families.
We have learned the lesson of lost love through death
or divorce and have come to know the sting of
loneliness.
We have experienced the tension of financial shortage
and the threat of economic collapse.
Despite our pain, or in part because of it, we remain
hopeful, faithful and grateful for your love.
For you have given us much and taken little.
You have sacrificed the root of Jesse so we may flower
and blossom.
You have helped us find among the ashes a sprig of
life,
something brave and adamant about new hope,
something that pushes up through the barren soil of
gloom,
something that refuses to die, to quit, to let death
have the last word.
Is it not, O Lord, the Word of Life, the Word made
Flesh, the Word we come to worship with heart and
mind?
Is it not Jesus the Christ, in whose name we pray?
Amen.

As We Gather (2)

O Lord of our Lives, you come to us as softly as a
child's footsteps and whisper in our ears that the
morning has broken and you have created this day for
worship.
You call us to rise from our sleep and join the
gathering of the faithful,
to enter your house with anticipation and hope,
to join hands with others who share our humanity and
our faith in your love,
to come before you with singing and prayer.
We pray for young families experiencing the joy, wonder
and worry of their first child;
we pray for parents adjusting to their children growing
up, leaving the home and making a life of their own;
we pray for those who have lived for so many years
they must now watch the passing of good friends;
and we pray for all who have gathered here that we
may once again find the strength we need for the living
of our days and hear again the song of hope, the faith
of the ages.
Draw near to us, O Lord, even as we draw near to you.
Amen.

Celebration Of God's Grace And Love (1)

Great God of Love, your abundant grace makes our lives
graceful — freely lived and freely given.
We claim our adoption as sons and daughters of God
not because we are worthy but because you give us
worth.
You unfasten the bonds that hold us back from becoming
a child of God,
a disciple of Christ,
a friend to those who suffer,
          those who are afraid,
          those who have lost hope.
You shatter the illusions of our self-importance
and challenge us to do something truly important:
to help a hurting child,
to listen to a broken heart,
to visit a person of age confined to a coffin-like
room,
to hold the hand of a person sick and dying,
to hand a bowl of soup to the hungry and homeless.
For you have given us the grace of love,
the word of liberation,
the promise of re-creation,
the power of healing.
You are the God who not only dances with us in the
meadow and kisses us with your morning sun
but sits with us in the darkness,
stays with us in our despair,
shivers with us through the cold, troubled night,
stands beside us in our pain, grief and sorrow.
O Giver of Life, may we pass along your gift of love.

Celebration Of God's Grace And Love (2)

O Generous God, your gifts abound and, at times,
overwhelm us with the weight of their love.
How often, O Lord, we have come to you with our empty
cups that have been poured out to others
and you fill them to overflowing with compassion,
renewed strength, continuous courage, healthy hope,
the will to go on.
Forgive us, O Lord, for our faltering faith;
fearing that by releasing some of our resources we
will jeopardize our future.
Help us not to be captives of the obsession for
security but to put our trust in you, Giver of all
great gifts!
For we know, Lord, though we do not always receive
what we want, you continually supply what we need.
And for that we are thankful!
We celebrate the joy you place in our hearts
as we participate in the divine act of giving a cup
of cool water to the thirsty. Amen.

Celebration Of God's Grace And Love (3)

O Great Composer of our lives, Conductor of the
symphony of spirits, we sing our praise to you.
From the "Gloria in Excelsis" of the Bethlehem angels
to the final "Amen" of human suffering,
we have heard your song rising like a crescendo in
our hearts.
O Lord, you have taught us to sing a new song,
a song of love and joy,
but the world has wandered off key.
Our voices have become flat and listless in our song
of justice
and too sharp and shrill with self-concern.
We would rather sing solos
than harmonize with your choir.
How patiently you tutor us!
How persistently you rehearse our song until it blends
with your divine anthem.
Your grace is so generous,
your love so gentle that our hearts burst with
"Alleluias" and our voices sing out your timeless
prayer. Amen.

Celebration Of God's Grace And Love (4)

God of our fathers and mothers,
Lord of our sons and daughters,
you roar like a lion
and speak with a lamb's voice.
Sometimes you murmur something to our minds.
Sometimes you converse with our hearts.
But we know when you have been near.
For suddenly, we are struck with an original thought,
or we glimpse a bold, new vision,
or the solution we have sought so long becomes
apparent.
You work secretly and quietly in the deepest regions
of our consciousness until, just at the right moment,
you reveal a new insight, a fresh concept.
We think it is our own
and you let us enjoy our self-deception.
But have you ever chuckled with parental delight at
our excitement in discovering a brilliant, unique
idea lurking in our heads?
O Lord, you are the Word that informs our words,
that gives them life and lift.
When you speak, the whole world shimmers with creative
energy and sparkling expectation!
When you listen, the over-burdened find relief,
the lost find their way,
the confused discover clarity,
the lonely find a friend.
Teach us to speak softly and listen with love.
Teach us to hear the silence of your presence and
to recognize your voice.
And teach us to pray the words that create community
and bring new life. Amen.

Celebration Of God's Grace And Love (5)

Holy God, Lord of Love, you know us better than anyone,
even better than we know ourselves.
When we were being formed in the womb,
your creative energy supported us.
As we were born into the world,
you breathed the breath of life into us.
You watched us grow through childhood
like a devoted mother, keeping us within your protection.
We are your children.
You call us by name.
Even as our legs grow long and our hair grows gray
we remain children of God, progeny of your patience
and long-suffering.
O God of grumpy grandparents,
possessive parents,
taunting teenagers,
careless children
and bawling infants,
you love us just the way we are
while encouraging us to become more than that.
O God, if you never overlooked our selfishness, pride
and greed could any survive?
But you do forgive us and for that we are grateful.
Your tears of sorrow wash away the sin of our past.
Your smile brightens our morning with renewed hope.
We hope that, perhaps, today we will find the courage
to forgive those who have wronged us.
Perhaps, today we will feel the warmth of compassion
instead of the heat of contempt.
Perhaps, even today we will be able to love ourselves
as you love us
and so love our neighbors as Jesus taught us. Amen.

Celebration Of God's Grace And Love (6)

O God of all good gifts, blend your love and justice
into our lives.
Make your will known to us in personal ways at special
times.
Help us to discover the unique gifts you have bestowed
on each of us to use in your service.
For we know some of us are called to be preachers,
teachers, elders and deacons.
But some are called to engineer policies and procedures
that are fair and faithful.
Some are called to examine our stewardship and to
find ways to stimulate its growth;
some are called to welcome people at the doors of
our sanctuary and to assist them in finding their
way;
some are called to dream dreams of ambitious projects
for extending and deepening our ministry to people
near and far;
and some are called to design strategies and organize
people to carry out those dreams.
Some find their place in calling on the sick,
hospitalized and imprisoned;
some are called to a ministry of art and
beautification;
some are called to spread the excitement of a growing
church with friends and neighbors;
and some are called to prepare the banquets and the
meals that enliven and enrich our fellowship events.
Some are called to sing loud and joyfully, even when they miss
the key;
some are called to listen to another's sorrow, to
encourage a faltering soul, to create a warm, positive
environment wherever they walk.
May we celebrate our differences as we give honor
and dignity to each part of Christ's body.
For we all worship one Lord, celebrate one baptism
and rejoice in the birth of the Spirit in our hearts
and in our community of faith. Amen.

Confessions Of The Community (1)

How wonderful are your ways, O Lord,
how marvelous are your gifts of grace.
You give to us not as we deserve but out of that love
which knows no bounds.
Daily we test your patience, your endurance, your
long-suffering.
Again and again we betray your trust and violate
your covenant of love, peace, justice.
We love too little,
want too much;
give only what is convenient,
take all we can;
expect more from others
than we do from ourselves;
grieve at our own loss
but extend little compassion toward people we do not
know who lose so much of the little they have gained.
How long, O Lord, can you forgive us?
How long, can you overlook our sin?
Straighten the backbone of our beliefs,
strengthen our resolve,
deepen our commitment to your way
so that the roots of faith will reach the center of
our hearts.
Then, to betray you would betray the very essence
of who we are!
We believe.
Help our unbelief — our unwillingless to trust
completely in your word and your way.
We love.
Help us to love more,
to love in larger circles,
to love beyond love's comfort
to love's challenge. Amen.

Confessions Of The Community (2)

O Giver of every good and perfect gift,
we thank you for the gift of life,
the freedom of worship
and the invitation to share in your love.
If you never overlooked our sins, Lord, who could
survive?
But you do forgive us and for that we revere you.
You call us to courageous discipleship
but come to us when we fall short.
You offer us the heart of Jesus
but we often choose the cunning of Judas.
We take credit for our accomplishments
and blame you for our disappointments.
Still, you won't give up on us!
You continue to believe in us
until we come to believe in you
and accept the gift of love,
the promise of your steadfast presence,
the power of your compassion and courage.
Empty our cups of poisonous pride and pour into our
hearts and minds the sweet wine of wonder and worship,
gratitude and grace,
humility and hope.
And teach us to hear and believe the good news of
Jesus Christ. Amen.

Confessions Of The Community (3)

O God, we pray for that love which is patient and
kind, which calls us out of our pettiness and pain,
which keeps us from casting stones at the weaknesses
of our friends,
which waits and grows not tired of waiting.
Remind us that this is the love of your Spirit.
It is the love Jesus taught us.
It is the love we desire to receive but are hesitant
to extend.
Grant us grace to impart this love to others.
Grant us patience with the afflictions of the very
old, the obnoxiousness of the very young,
the arrogance of youth and
the pride of the middle-aged.
Grant us the love which is kind to all persons
without concern for what they can or cannot do for
us . . . or to us.
May we give as we have been given or would wish to
be given:
to love patiently, forgivingly
and forever kind. Amen.

Confessions Of The Community (4)

O Great Covenantal God,
who continues to seek a relationship of integrity
and reliability from his people,
we know you have kept your promises.
We are a people who have been freed from bondage:
the bondage of guilt,
the bondage of sin and destruction,
the bondage of pride and self-righteousness.
And we have been welcomed into that promised land
of your love which gives nourishment and new life
to our hungry souls.
But we are people of broken promises,
people who are not able to fulfill the expectations
you place on us:
the expectation of enduring, unconditional love,
the expectation of forgiving others as we are forgiven,
the expectation of telling the truth,
the expection of working unfailingly for justice,
the expectation of being your peacemakers.
We come to you with our brokenness, O God,
because we know the pain and devastation of broken
promises, broken hearts, broken homes.
We ask for that healing and forgiveness which only
you can provide.
Sometimes the only promise we can keep is the promise
of humility and remorse as we seek that close reunion
with your Spirit once again.
Help us, O Lord, to learn to keep our commitments
to each other and to you. Amen.

Confessions Of The Community (5)

Creator God, Architect of Life and Love,
we enjoy the resurrection of each new day,
standing in your light,
basking in the warmth of your love.
You bring order out of chaos — not only on the
cosmological scale but on the common plane as well.
You call us to center our hearts in your Son Jesus,
to build back our shattered lives on the sure
foundation of our Lord's forgiveness and gift of faith.
You design a blueprint for each of our lives on which
we can construct great and beautiful edifices of
discipleship.
And yet, we continually choose to erect our values
on the sandy soil of selfishness,
the shifting stones of wealth,
the sliding mud of mean pride.
O God, save us from our foolishness,
our childish attempts to cut corners in the
construction of our lives,
to find the easy way,
the cheap solution.
Teach us the cost of discipleship and the mature wisdom
that seeks your vision and guidance. Amen.

Confessions Of The Community (6)

Searching and Calling God,
you follow us to the ends of the earth.
You walk with us through valleys of pain, sadness
and disappointment.
You stand by us when all others desert us
and you fill our loneliness with your Spirit.
Every day you call us from our dark sleep with your
celestial light.
You leave your footprint on the scarlet sunset.
You surround us with your love.
How can we be so blind that we cannot see you?
How can our hearts be so cold that we cannot sense
your presence?
What more can we ask than that the Word become flesh
and dwell among us?
And it has!
Your word is spoken in every act of human kindness,
every courageous defense of the poor and powerless,
every struggle toward peace and reconciliation,
every gathering of two or three in your name.
Why then is the world so deaf?
Why can we not hear your word of love that sings in
our hearts,
lifts our spirits to hope and leads us on the path
of righteousness?
Give us faith to see and to hear your word as it is
spoken to us and spoken through us. Amen.

Confessions Of The Community (7)

O God of Endless Time, we rejoice in your inseparable
love!
We find assurance in your constant compassion.
Though we hide from you, we want to be found.
Though we flee from the sound of your voice, we seek
our Master's call.
In this tension between me-and-Thee, we trust your
will to triumph.
Like children, we sometimes demand to go our own way.
But, like children, when we stumble and fall and our
dreams lie broken and scattered on the ground, we
hope you are there to catch our tears, to bathe our
wounds and lift us again to our feet.
Remind us how frail we are and how few our days on
this planet, so we will cease to cling to our false
fortress and learn to soar with the flight of your
Spirit.
You have set before us the Kingdom of Heaven;
we choose the cradle of conceit.
You place before us the commitment of your cross;
we choose the comfort of compromise.
You tell us a story of love's victory over death;
we write histories of war and suffering.
O God, forget us not!
We pray you will not give up on us though we so often
let you down.
We dare to ask for forgiveness once again,
to seek adoption into discipleship,
to be included as a member of your family of faith.
Transform us from rebellious adolescent to a
child of God. Amen.

For The Word Of God (1)

O God of Truth, your Word has reached us through the
mouths of your prophets, the pen of your scribes and
the witness of your faithful community down through
the ages.
May your Word be written on our hearts and spring
forth from our mouths.
May it become alive in our acts of love,
of caring for the weak and powerless,
of healing broken relationships and broken hearts.
May your Word become the foundation for our words,
our thoughts,
our conversations,
our concerns.
May the good news which we have heard be shared with
others that they too may experience your liberating
hope.
Keep us from growing content with the gifts we have
received and teach us to be generous, to be bold,
to be loving, to be faithful.
Make your prophetic message heard through what we
say and do in the name of Jesus Christ, our Lord.
Amen.

For The Word Of God (2)

O Word of Life, you speak and out of nothing
your creation is born.
You speak and out of darkness a light shines,
a brilliant light that the darkness cannot extinguish.
The fire of faith rages on
consuming cynicism and doubt,
melting our hearts and pouring them out into the
hollow cups of a thirsty world.
O Word of Love, you speak and
two become one.
You speak and two or three or more
become a community of Christ.
The silence of separation is broken with the sacrifice
of self-interest
and love that is lasting and healing
is made possible.
O Word of Hope,
speak to us and through us your words of everlasting
life. Amen.

For The Word Of God (3)

How precious is your Word, O Lord!
How rare and unique is its power to transform, to
heal, to render hope.
Your Word calls us out of
our sleep,
our hopelessness,
our contrived existence
to something real,
something true,
something lasting.
Teach us to hear, O Lord,
to recognize your voice,
to respond with great expectation to your call to
worship, to faith, to prayer.
Teach us to see, O Lord, with the eyes of faith, to
sense your presence.
Give us the courage of your vision, to see our lives
through your eyes in order to spot honest hurt
and redeeming hope.
May we not keep your love a secret
but proclaim it to all the world
with joy and gratitude. Amen.

For The Word Of God (4)

God of Creation, Author of Truth, we thank you for
the word inscribed in stone;
it is our map through the madness of this world,
our way through the wilderness of doubt, fear, grief.
We thank you for the word you have placed in our
mouths; we have tasted your truth and know it is good;
we have taken and eaten as you commanded.
We thank you for the word you have written on our
hearts: the word of faith,
          the word of hope,
          the word of love.
And we praise you with glad and grateful songs for
your Living Word:
the Word made flesh;
the Word that dwells among us and within us;
the Word that gives integrity to our speech, depth
to our spirits, courage to our hearts.
Help us to hear and understand the language of our
Lord, the good news of the gospel and the promise
of the prayer he taught us to say together. Amen.

Advent (1)

O God, it is the Season of Advent
and we are waiting . . .
waiting for love to rekindle its flame in the hollow
of our hearts;
waiting for that peace which is beyond comprehension
to quiet our troubled thoughts;
waiting for justice to become a word that is constantly
on our lips and faithfully in our actions;
waiting for the Light of Life to brighten our steps
in the dark winter nights.
Come quickly, Jesus, and lift the shadow of our vision.
Come quickly, Lord, and coax us out of our hiding
places.
Place us in the midst of the hungry.
Put us face-to-face with the lonely.
Remind us of how much we have to give to those who
have so little.
And keep us hopeful, O Lord, even when wars and rumors
of wars threaten to undo us, paralyze our faith
and cripple our creativity.
Give us courage to live out your message of
reconciliation and kindness.
May the love which we seek
be the love which we share.
May the forgiveness we need
be the forgiveness we offer to others.
Keep us from the arrogance of single-minded nationalism
or self-righteous religiosity.
Cleanse our minds from the real enemies:
fear, prejudice, guilt, hostility and pride.
And return to our thoughts the vision of the gentleness
that became a world-changing power.
May we not only believe in your love
but live it every day in everything we say or do,
so that the One on whom we wait will be born anew
in the world. Amen.

Advent (2)

"Come, thou long-expected Jesus!"
As we wait for the One who has already come, prepare
our hearts and minds to be receptive, O God.
Build a manger within us that will cradle the Christ.
Create within us a spiritual space that will welcome
your Holy Spirit.
May we not wait as strangers in a bus depot
who stand alone,
ignoring each other's stare,
ignorant of another's pain,
consumed by private concern.
But may we wait like a family gathered in a
hospital room anticipating the arrival of a child,
a brother, a sister.
May we share familiar stories of our common past,
remembering those times together when mutual comfort
made our toxic tears taste sweet and warm,
when our joy came dancing up to our mouths and we
rejoiced with singing and laughter,
when we encouraged each other to be strong, to be
brave and to hope our way through the night storm
until your calm morning light returned.
O make us as family, kind Father, that welcomes Jesus
as Lord!
Amen.

Advent (3)

As we approach this season of Advent, O God,
remind us who we are and what you can become for us.
May the sweet music, the lovely colors and designs
create in our hearts a new sense of purpose and
excitement about our future.
May your spirit of forgiveness become a mitigating
force in our lives that will bring us closer to those
people who have drifted away from us;
allow us to see through the distraction of their
hostility into the fears of their inner lives.
How blessed is your name, O God, especially when it
becomes interpreted into acts of self-giving love.
May we find a way this Advent season
to light a candle of hope in someone's life,
to be a source of healing to someone in emotional
distress,
to bring company and delight to one who is isolated
and alone,
to discover the playful and creative child in a person
we thought too old
or to recognize the wisdom of Solomon in a child we
thought too young.
May we rededicate ourselves to the work of your church
and the worship of your people.
Restore in us the excitement of the first Christmas
which brought forth the immediacy of your
healing love and the hope of your everlasting life.
Amen.

Advent (4)

Despite the hustle and hassle of Christmas,
O Lord, may your holiness shine through.
May the demands of this season on our energy and time
not diminish our devotion to its purpose.
O God, let your Word rise above the clatter and
confusion of our words.
Let your truth overcome the falseness around us,
your shining stars prevail above the neon lights of
the city.
May your warm love blanket the chill of the cold night
as we remember, Emmanuel — Lord with us!
O Christ of Bethlehem, we open our hearts to you.
But you will find no rest within.
For our spirits are troubled by a world trembling
on the brink of destruction and
our guilt at doing little or nothing to avoid it.
We suffer over the tormenting spread of hunger,
lives that are ravaged by disease,
nations that arm for war in this season of peace.
So come, Child of Bethlehem, into the rage deep within
us.
Still the storm.
Calm the conflict.
Quiet our fears.
Then send us the peace and confidence to travel
beyond comfort to comforting action,
beyond inertia to hope-filled effort,
beyond excuse to commitment.
Blend your Spirit with our prodigal soul
and lead us back to your straight and narrow path
of courageous compassion.
Share with us the obedient faith of that young woman
you chose to bear your Son
so our question will be transformed into obedience,
our, "How can this be?" may become
"Let it be, according to your word!" Amen.

Advent (5)

Lights, laughter and warm fires
remind us that we are nearing that special day,
O God: the day of hope,
      the day of wonder,
      the night of promise.
May the surprises of this season enrich our families.
May those without families hear of your family of
faith and come home to the embrace of acceptance,
warmth and love.
Though tinseled trees, over-stuffed red suits and
holly-bedecked store windows clamor for our attention,
may your vision of a new world
made perfect by love's light
never be overshadowed.
Christ Jesus, we dare to think of you as a child,
needing the protection of a young mother.
Such a humble image forces us to our knees;
it defies our imagination;
it betrays all previous notions of power and majesty.
You took the risk of coming to us in weakness,
vulnerable as an infant,
so we could learn of your strength.
Because of you, O Lord, we find strength in our
weakness,
power in our helplessness,
joy in our sorrow,
music in our silence
and friend in our loneliness.
Continue surprising us, O God,
when our faith becomes fixed,
and continue encouraging us to follow our dreams.
May our dreams be yours, O Lord,
even in this Holy Season — the season of our lives.
Amen.

Christmas (1)

How great is your love, O God,
to send us your Son.
Though your Church has waited four weeks for the coming
of Christmas,
many of us have waited the coming of Christ
for years.
Some of us have forgotten what it is we are waiting
for.
We have lost patience and turned to lesser gods that
deliver instant pleasure.
We have lost faith and begun believing in boisterous
gods to protect us — gods of death and destruction.
We have lost hope and become cynical and hard
rather than face our fear.
Christ of compassion
come into our hearts this Christmas.
Be born in us today.
Provide us that new life that can only come from your
Spirit:
the new life of faith that is steadfast and sure;
the new life of hope that endures beyond the feasible;
the new life of love that increases as it is given
away.
Because of our stubborn blindness,
we have waited too long for your love.
Open our eyes that we may see your love
which has waited much longer
for us. Amen.

Christmas (2)

It is the Day of Joy, O Loving God,
when our memory of your gift of life becomes vivid
and real.
The millions of paths and highways
we have chosen to follow
converge at Bethlehem where a small child brings
comfort to generations of believers.
We pause at the manger to hear a new message and
receive creative directions for the living of our
lives.
For unto us a child is born;
unto us a Son is given.
And a peace that is incomprehensible has entered the
world!
The stream of history has deviated from the integrity
of the gospel.
Our nation has witnessed the destruction of false
prophets;
our fathers and grandfathers smelled the stench of
death wrought by war after senseless war;
hungry and starving people have grown weary as their
desperate pleas for human compassion have gone
unheeded.
How far we have wandered from your path of
righteousness!
What great distance have we strayed from your cross
of compassion!
Comfort your people, O God,
not with cheap grace,
but with the assurance that true discipleship matters
and has impact on human suffering, loneliness and
fear.
We come to you
because you have come to us. Amen.

Christmas (3)

The bells of Christmas ring in our ears, O Lord,
even as your love rings true in our hearts.
For unto us a child is born
and our barren lives are filled with great joy!
Unto us a Son is given
and our dark world is bathed in his light.
He takes upon himself the government of our minds
and we sense a purpose and direction in our lives.
He is our Wonderful Counselor,
the Mighty God,
the Prince of Peace,
who saves us from our self-deceit,
our desperation,
our paralyzing guilt,
our consuming grief,
our fear of death
and our fear of life.
O God, who speaks to the humble the word of hope,
open our eyes that we may see the brilliant revelation
of the Child who was born for us all,
the one who takes away the sins of the world
and brings us life that overcomes death.
He gives us love that heals the wounds of our past.
He gives voice to our carols of joy! Amen.

Christmas (4)

O Bright and Shining God,
who comes to us in the Morning Star,
awaken our eyes to the gift of your Spirit.
Help us to see through eyes of faith
the great and glorious advent of everlasting love and universal
forgiveness.
Reach into the depths of our hearts and seize our
conviction and commitment to your word and work.
May we labor with joy in service to your kingdom:
that the stranger to our community may be received
as a friend;
that those from faraway places may enjoy the warmth
of our homes and our hearts;
that the lonely and distressed may discover a family
who cares
so that every knee may one day bow down and every
tongue confess you as Lord and Savior.
Blessed God, we thank you for the Word made flesh,
which not only dwelled among us,
but resides within us — where blood and bone come
together to form a human being softened by the word
of compassion,
humbled by the word of pardon,
strengthened by the hope of salvation
and encouraged by the promise of peace.
May we be an instrument of your peace, O God, and
a disciple of your love. Amen.

Loving God, in the warmth of the virgin's womb
the Holy Child waits to be born.
In the cradle of our hearts, Jesus Christ waits to be reborn.
Is it possible, O God, that we too could experience
rebirth this night?
Is it possible that a head full of questions could
find peace on a night such as this?
Is it possible a heart burdened by the shame of
yesterday could find release from guilt, restoration
of esteem, confidence for the future?
Your messenger, Gabriel, announced to Mary that "with
God, nothing is impossible."
If this is true, Lord, then give us
faith that goes beyond fear,
belief that overcomes doubt,
hope that shines like a star in the darkest night
of our desolation.
O Wonderful Counselor, lead us by the hand through
the confusion of our lives;
Mighty God, give us power and courage to live your
love;
Everlasting Father, comfort us when we come running
to you bleeding and hurt.
O Prince of Peace, quiet the passions of this warring
world,
the conflict in our communities,
the struggle in our hearts.
May your peace restore our hope,
your presence return our joy! Amen.

Christmas (6)

O Peaceful and Quiet God,
you arrive in the stillness of the night and are
greeted by those who have been patiently waiting.
It is the fullness of time,
    the acceptable time,
    the eternal now,
    the moment of ultimate meaning.
It is a time when your radiant light reveals our
carefully kept secrets,
our well-hidden faults,
our character blemishes,
and our desperate illusions.
It is a time to face ourselves and our past
and make important decisions about our future.
Must we continue to be the victim of carelessness,
apathy, self-centered preoccupations, ancient grudges,
destructive guilt?
Or have you created this moment for us to choose
who is to be Lord of our lives?
On this night is your power sufficient for us to
collect the courage it takes to let go of peevish
thoughts, irritating behaviors, controlling feelings
and experience once again,
or perhaps for the first time,
that indescribable sense of release and relief that
comes when we say, "Yes!" to the gift of your Spirit?
Give wings to our timid faith that we may soar like
eagles above the valley of anguish and the ravines
of anger.
We want so much to believe in the magic of Christmas,
the possibilities of love,
the peace of mind that comes with a life of purpose
and direction.
Grant to us, O God, the gift of faith that is free
of self-limitation and open to the birth of Christ
in heart and mind. Amen.

Christmas (7)

Tonight the people of the world are silent, O God,
listening for the sound of love to ring out in their
hearts.
We have waited so long
hoping for our Savior,
groaning for justice,
wishing for peace.
And yet, the sounds we hear are the whispered prayers
of hostages unjustly held captive,
the explosion of the gifts of war, the packages of
death,
the mumbling of the weak and hungry,
the desperate cry of abandoned children, forgotten
grandparents, grief-stricken survivors.
Can love be born tonight, O God?
Can we alone, or together, create a song of hope
that will carry beyond the decorated walls of
overflowing sanctuaries?
Can we produce a flicker of light in the deafening
blight of evil?
Has it really been 2,000 years since you showed us
how?
With a humble birth,
     a quiet, persistent ministry,
     a courageous, self-giving lifestyle,
     an invincible, forgiving manner,
     a fearless facing of violence and corruption,
     a consistent awareness of the individual in the
crowd needing special attention, a tender touch . . .
and a faith that always found a place for prayer and
worship, obedience and commitment,
you, O Christ, have made peace possible,
love real and faith alive.
We thank you, God, for the Creative One,
the Artist of Heaven,
the One who taught us the power of poetry and prayer.
Amen.

Palm Sunday (1)

Down from the Mount of Olives you come, O Lord,
riding on a burro.
The path is steep and narrow
but still you come,
knowing that the same people who shout, "Hosanna!"
will one day demand, "Crucify Him!"
Still you come.
Your accusers lurk in the shadows of that great walled
city and yet you ride down main street.
Is there no sacrifice too great for you love,
no fear too crippling?
You sit like a general upon your humble steed,
but where is your army?
Like a king, you ride before the cheering crowd.
O foolish king, where is your kingdom?
We would be your subjects but we cannot find your
kingdom.
We look in Jerusalem.
It is not there.
We look to governments.
None profess you as Sovereign Lord.
We ascend to the heavens and are met by infinite space.
Where then do we find your Spirit,
O Loving King?
Our voices praise you, singing, "Alleluia! Alleluia!"
and our mouths profess, "Jesus as Lord."
Only then
do our hearts burn within us.
Only then
do we feel the piercing penetration of your
crown of thorns
and fall on our knees
before the King of Hearts! Amen.

Palm Sunday (2)

Great and Glorious God, we join the timeless,
hallelujah chorus in singing and shouting our praise
for the entry of Christ
into our lives.
To each of us Palm Sunday has become a unique,
personal experience of joy and celebration
for the triumph of love over hatred,
servanthood over oppressive power,
cooperation over exploitation,
unity over divisiveness,
peace over the noisy confusion of our time
and hope over the debilitation of fear.
We know now that to follow the parade of self-giving
compassion leads almost certainly to a cross of
contempt and brutality.
And yet, we follow.
We follow the One who calls us forward to face the
turmoil and tempest with confidence in his transforming
power.
We follow him because he once pursued us
into the forest of our fear, the jungle of our savage
soul and led us tenderly into a clearing,
out to a calm place of quiet rest and renewal.
We follow even though the path is frustrating and
treacherous because it is the only way, the only truth,
the only life.
And because he leads us.
God, forgive us for stumbling and pulling away from
your grasp.
May we choose to march in your parade with courage
and go where it takes us, trusting in the power of
your Holy Spirit. Amen.

Palm Sunday (3)

O Palm Sunday God, who enters our heart with leaping
hosannas, we rejoice and are glad to welcome your
entry.
Come into our city and restore humility and honor.
Come into our church and transform us with eagerness
and enthusiasm.
Come into our families and unite us as a supportive
community.
Come into each of our lives and drive out the
"moneychangers" in our minds:
the passion for position and prestige;
the long-term guilt that eats away at our confidence
and self-worth;
the bitter loneliness that keeps us from caring.
God of Palm Sunday, point us to Good Friday.
Give us the courage to die to self-justification,
to pseudo-symbols of worship,
to false faces in the crowd,
to meaningless endeavor,
to expectations of magical cures for complex human
struggles
and to apathy which turns its face from
pain.
Give us the courage to care,
to know your love in our hearts
and to rise to your expectations of us,
even as we ride in the parade of faith. Amen.

Palm Sunday (4)

God of Grace and Glory, we praise you for the
sacrificial love of Jesus Christ,
who was victorious only because of his obedience.
He came not to be served but to serve.
He came not as a man of war but as the Prince of Peace.
He rode into Jerusalem with shouts of "Hosanna!"
For he came to save us from the captivity of our own
corruption, self-deceit, greed.
Free us, Son of David, from the fears that haunt us,
the sorrow that finds no solace,
the guilt that plagues our thoughts and destroys our
self-worth.
Free us from doubts that debilitate,
contentment that converts to apathy,
cynicism that makes cowards of us all.
May we not stand idly by as your parade passes.
Rather, may we march with you and ride tall in
humility.
We rejoice in the invitation to join the grand
procession of peace and justice,
to walk with him who comes
in the name of the Lord. Amen.

Palm Sunday (5)

Great God of joy and celebration, we lift our songs
and voices with gladness for that great parade of
hope.
He has come to our city, our streets, our homes, our
hearts and left nothing unchanged.
We have been touched by his grace and felt his
friendship in our suffering.
For we, too, have known the pain of betrayal,
the shiver of fear in the garden,
the frustration of unfair systems, unjust laws,
the abandonment of close friends in a time of need.
So we clap for joy at his arrival.
We shout "Hosanna" at his coming.
We dance the dance of freedom.
We sing the songs of liberation.
For his love is everlasting;
his forgiveness is sure;
his hand is strong and will not let us lie where we
fall.
Thank you, God, for Palm Sunday,
for festive occasions,
for the laughter of children, both young and old,
for sounds of cymbals and drums, trumpets and
tambourines,
but most of all for your Son, Jesus Christ,
the King of Kings,
the one who brings healing and health to broken lives,
crippled bodies,
failed dreams,
tortured minds
and starving souls.
May we take this parade of hope to friend, family
and stranger and share our love,
our gifts,
our courage
and our certainty of a God who cares. Amen.

Easter (1)

How beautiful are the lilies of the field, O God;
how gracefully do they sway in the wind
and trustingly open their soft petals to the rising
sun.
It is Easter
and our hearts are glad!
It is Easter
and memories of fear and denial,
loneliness and death are remodeled
by the gift of life,
the significance of love
and the peace which goes beyond human events
to the very heartbeat of existence.
It is Easter
and we celebrate the return of the lost one,
the reunion with him who was separated from us.
We who are lost and alienated
look to him as our hope for forgiveness,
our light through dark thoughts,
our joy in the morning,
our friend for the journey.
Touch us with your truth, O God.
Make your way known to us,
bring us to your life, Great God,
which is abundant in power
and overflowing with wonder.
The Prophet has come;
the prophecy is fulfilled;
the promise is sure;
the hope is eternal.
It is Easter
and we celebrate the Light of Life,
the Lord of us all. Amen

Easter (2)

Holy Father of the New Day,
we join trumpet and bell in singing your glory.
Our victory song springs forth from the new life you
have given us in the Resurrection of your Beloved
Son.
We sing to the power of love which overcomes the powers
of violence and vengeance.
We sing to our baptism and for the new self that rises
up out of the ashes of the old.
We sing to the Bread of Life that satisfies what we
once feared was an insatiable spiritual hunger.
We sing to the cup of salvation that pours into our
thirsty souls the life blood of the cross.
We sing to the joy of eternal life
which gives our living
abundance
and our dying
hope.
And we sing to the kingdom of God in our hearts
in the name of our Risen Lord, Jesus Christ. Amen.

Easter (3)

Resurrection God,
you bring life to that which was dead.
You bring joy to our sorrow,
comfort for our tears.
You call us out of the grave of greed,
the tomb of isolation and indifference
to come alive with love,
to share what we have and who we are,
to become your bearers of new life.
Where darkness has shrouded hope,
may your light shine through us.
Where sickness in our relationships creates conflict
and disease in our bodies destroys courage,
may your healing hand be upon us and work through
us.
O God,
make us brave disciples who will not accept the
dominance of death
but will work with you,
believe in you,
hold steadfast to you
as you create new life, new joy, new love in and around
us by the power of of your Son, our Risen Lord,
Jesus Christ. Amen.

Easter (4)

Great God of Easter Morning,
your brilliant light breaks forth from the darkness.
Another day has been created.
Another hope restored!
You refuse to let us sleep an eternal night.
Your Son comes to us in the morning.
His luminous radiance fills our private rooms with
love.
Our eyes can remain closed no more.
We are aroused from our slumber to the promise of
a new day:
a day of living and loving,
a day of breathing and walking,
a day of laughter and joy,
a day of trying on the love you have made
and giving it away to those in need.
For this is the day that you have made!
A Day of Resurrection:
a day to recover the faith by which we live,
to put on the clothes of compassion, the garments
of grace,
to place in our pockets the fortune of forgiveness
and to go out into the world with the courage of
Christ,
a courage that dares to say to a menacing, hostile
world, "I love you!"
Resurrect in each of us, O Lord,
the power of your Spirit embodied in your gathered
community of faith. Amen.

Thanksgiving Sunday (1)

God of our pilgrim parents,
we thank you for the legacy of this land:
the freedom of voice, of prayer, of praise;
the opportunity to work, to learn, to grow;
the respect for each person's conscience;
the reverence for life.
O Merciful God,
we are thankful that you have called us together to
your house of prayer and that as we depart
we return to our own homes — shelter from the wind,
protection from harm's way.
For those families who sleep in our streets and huddle
in our alleyways
we ask that your mercy in our hearts will help them
find a home.
Compassionate God,
we are grateful that you have called us to your table
to break bread and share one cup;
and we thank you for ample food on our tables and
water to drink.
For those families who scrape the barren dust for
seeds, who daily search for a bite to eat, who walk
miles for a cup of water
we ask that your compassion in our hearts will help
them find enough to eat and drink.
Loving Lord,
we praise you for calling us together into a family
of faith, a community of caring, of comfort, of
support.
We ask that your love in our hearts will help us to
reach out to the lonely, the isolated, the people
who hide in fear or pain
and to share Christ's love with them,
invite them into Christ's community
and surround them with a fellowship of faith, of hope,
of healing.
Thank you God,
for our lives, for your love,
for our families, for your church,
for our friends and for your Son, our Living Lord.
Amen.

Thanksgiving Sunday (2)

Creator God, Lord of the harvest,
we praise you for the good earth,
for the gifts of life and love,
for the fellowship of friends, the support of family,
the caring concern of your congregation.
We are grateful for the freedom of worship and work,
the opportunity to grow and learn
and to share ourselves with others.
We thank you for the help which comes to us in times
of trouble and pain:
a friendly visit,
a listening ear,
a funny card,
a warm letter,
a long-distance call,
a bouquet of flowers,
a book of inspiration.
Thank you, Lord, for the ordinary days of simple
pleasures and quiet charm;
and for those extraordinary days of laughing and
weeping when the drama and depth of life
touch and warm our hearts.
Forgive us, Lord, for prayers of petition that are
too long
and prayers of praise that are
too short.
May gratitude for the grace you have given us in the
love of Jesus Christ reign supreme in our lives and
fall frequently from our lips.
Thanks be to you, God, for the gift of your Son,
Jesus Christ. Amen.

Mother's Day (1)

O Great and Wonderful God,
you are long-suffering and forgiving.
Except for your patience, how could we hope to grow?
Except for your pardon, how could we escape the bondage
of our guilt?
Except for your comfort, how could we search the
darkness for a glimmer of hope?
You gather us around your skirts and keep us close
to your side.
You call and we come running.
Your difficult instruction is graced by your
gentleness.
How tenderly you support us in the palm of your hand.
How softly you speak your words of encouragement and
life.
You are the parent God who gathers all your children
back in your arms.
We who are parents look to you as counselor and friend.
We who are mothers know something of the joy of your
Son's birth:
the pride of showing off one's child to the world;
the care as he grows and matures and discovers his
destiny;
the sorrow and protective anger when he is discouraged
and rebuked, rejected and hurt;
and the painful, bitter tears at his suffering and
untimely death.
We wail with all the mothers of the world who have
lost their sons and daughters needlessly to the sin
and destruction of this world.
And we rejoice with all the mothers of the world
who having lost their children, found them;
who celebrate the victory of their child's life,
the triumph of their child's faith,
the depth of their child's love and thoughtfulness.
Amen.

Mother's Day (2)

O Mother God,
who has given us life through the birth pangs of the
cross,
nourish us with your tenderness,
restore us with your touch.
You gather us around your skirts and cradle us in
your arms.
O God, we know that adulthood does not dissolve our
childlike wonder nor our need for loving care.
We are grateful for your motherly affection
and for our earthly mothers.
We are thankful for the mothers of justice who have
raised our awareness of how sexism dehumanizes
everyone,
who have given birth to a refreshing sense of equality
and companionship in the power and promise of life
and who have found ways to reach through our protective
defenses and superficial roles to the heart of our
humanity.
We thank you for the mothers of our personal history,
who recall the stories of our childhood,
who remind us of who we are and the events that shaped
our adulthood,
who carry in their hearts the humor of our human
foibles, the joy of our curiosity, those first
discoveries of life's secrets and those proud, simple
achievements that only mothers remember.
And we thank you for our mothers who are no longer
with us: those who have passed from this life into
the next,
those who brighten your heavens after giving of
themselves in this life,
those whom we remember with affection. Amen.

Mother's Day (3)

God of Life, we come to you with glad hearts,
thankful for the return of warm weather, blue sky,
purple iris.
Today our gratitude is great for the tradition and
ritual that enlivened our childhood and made our
personal history memorable.
We are grateful for the cool winter nights warmed
by the taste of hot chocolate,
a crackling fireplace,
a tender touch on a child's smooth brow.
We are happy for the persistence of the parent who
roused us out of bed on Sunday mornings
insisting we wake up for worship and helped us shove
growing feet into the inflexible leather of new shoes.
And we are grateful for the parent who went with us
to church: to that fellowship of believers,
that community of saints,
that strange assortment of people from all walks of
life who found a unique friendship in the singing
of hymns, the sharing of prayers, the hearing of
sermons, the caring for those who sorrow.
For mothers, who found their way into our hearts with
patient instruction, incorrigible humor, courageous
concern and gentle, comforting hugs, we thank you
especially.
For mothers of children,
mothers of adults,
mothers borrowed by lonely, distressed people,
for all who have learned the motherly art of graceful
love,
we give you thanks, Lord.
And we praise you, O God, for teaching us how to be
good, kind and loving parents to all your children.
Amen.

Commissioning A Youth Mission Trip (1)

O Great God of justice and mercy,
you have called us to be a pilgrim people, to venture
into strange lands and combat our fears of the unknown,
the untried.
You bid us walk through the narrow gate,
to take the road less traveled:
the road of human pain and suffering;
the road of self-sacrifice;
the trailway of a courageous spirit.
Forgive our timidity, our reluctance to leave the
comfort of our familiar lifestyles and share the
difficult struggle of living that confronts most of
the world.
Open our ears that we may hear their cry;
open our hearts to pray with and for them;
open our mouths to admonish inequity and announce
the good news of your liberating love.
Thank you, Lord, for giving these young people a
vision, for calling them to a mission of hard toil
and helping hands.
As the hands of your Son were scarred by his work
of salvation,
so may the blisters and callouses on the hands of our
sons and daughters be a sign of their work of love.
Finally, we ask your blessing on all your children
who work for your kingdom on earth
and raise their hands together in prayer. Amen.

For Social Responsibility (1)

O Lord, we have seen your face
shining through the dark, wet eyes of African children
hungry for food;
the tight, fearful faces of wandering drifters
toughened by time and trouble;
the brown, dusty faces of Central Americans victimized
by tyranny, hoping for freedom;
the blank, blue walls, searching for the lost past.
Give us the courage of faith that reaches out and
makes a connection with the hungry, the stranger,
the old, the powerless.
May we touch and be touched by the pain and suffering
of this world.
May the tears of others flow down our cheeks.
May the terror which haunts the daily existence of
too many people make us restless.
May the isolation and loneliness of those imprisoned
by cages of steel or bodies diseased or worn out by
time drive us from contentment to contact.
May we rediscover the saving power of
a cup of cool water,
a loaf of bread,
a listening ear,
a shared hurt,
a gentle touch.
And may he, who turned the violence of our hands into
the possibility for healing,
embrace us with his love. Amen.

For Social Responsibility (2)

Spirit of the Living God, fall afresh on us.
Open our hearts to a far-reaching compassion that
extends around the world,
to the most obscure corners of this troubled planet.
Let us remember you are God of all people:
the beautiful and the homely;
the well-dressed and the naked;
the rich and the hungry;
the ones who speak loudly and those who barely utter
a word;
the ones who have bodies of steel and those whose
bodies are broken and bent;
the very young and the very old.
God of time and space,
give us time to grow up in your Spirit;
give us room to grow up in our faith
so that our ears may hear the knock at the door,
the cry for help,
the whimper of weakness,
the sigh of loneliness
and so our hands will reach out with the love of your
Son.
Teach us the meaning of this kind of love
which knows no boundary
and no second thoughts
but springs forth like a fountain.
And may the source of this love remember us
as we remember him in our responses of faithfulness.
Amen.

For Social Responsibilitiy (3)

O Lord, our lives are like a song out of tune,
lacking rhythm or harmony.
Our eyes have narrowed in vision from focusing too
long on self-concern; we lack periphery and depth.
Our hands have lost their creative freedom from holding
on too tightly to things of insignificance.
May we lose in order to find.
May we open our eyes and see the possibilities of
your Spirit;
may we lift our voices and sing, even in the face
of danger.
Blessed God, roll back the clouds and let the sun
shine brightly in our souls.
May your love penetrate the dullness of daily existence
and remind us of the joy which comes from reaching
higher than the shelf of selfishness to the one of
friendship, kindness, justice.
May your forgiveness challenge our arrogance and teach
us to give when it hurts,
to occasionally trust the opinion of others,
to yield to a different way of seeing and
understanding.
These are times that test the soul,
that call forth the courage of morality,
the integrity of truth,
the dignity of decency.
May we have the strength of committed Christians who
have known 2,000 years of suffering for justice,
of caring for the forgotten,
of seeking the lost.
And may we have that faith which finds power in the
unity of your everlasting love. Amen.

For Social Responsibility (4)

O Great God of Hope, your victorious trumpet sounds
the call to a ministry of social responsibility.
It is a melody of mystery, a silent symphony, a strange
new sound amid the clamor of the cults,
the lure of secularism
and the clatter of profiteers.
May the sharp cry of your Spirit call us to a sense
of wonder in a bored world,
to creativity in a tired community,
to faith in a skeptic's society,
to compassion in a self-centered age.
Lift heavy hearts and hopeless hands
to sing a new song,
to dance before the Lord,
to clap hands,
raise trumpets,
beat drums
and shout out loud:
"The Lord is with us!
He is in his holy temple!
His temple is in our hearts!
Praise be to God who has given life!
He is the Light of the world,
the Alpha and the Omega,
the beginning of hope,
the final meaning.
Jesus Christ is his name!"
Let us praise him with song and with prayer! Amen.

For Liberation (1)

From our prisons we shout, from our cages we cry,
"You are the Lord, giver of mercy;
You are the Christ, giver of mercy.
Have mercy on us, O God, and give us your grace."
Freeing God, within the framework of our lives we
hope to see hostages released;
we pray the criminally convicted will be made whole;
and we look for the day when you will liberate our
faith from the skepticism of our minds,
when you will free the love in our hearts to be fully
expressed in our mouths and our hands.
We hope for the day when the dying may be freed from
their fear of death
and the timid and bored may be released from
their fear of life.
Give us courage to believe, O God.
Give us faith to see beyond the webbing of our wire
fences the possibility of running in warm, yellow
meadows and sitting beside cool, blue waters.
Remind us of the power of our minds to see what we
want to see, hear what we want to hear, believe what
we want to believe.
May we set our eyes on you, O God.
May our ears hear the faint whisper of hope.
May we believe in him who refused to let his spirit
be crucified and his trust in God diminish
and who, even unto death, was able to say,
"Father, into thy hands I commit my spirit."
Now, O Lord, we commit ourselves to you. Amen.

For Liberation (2)

Out of the darkness we cry, O God!
We ask for endurance to carry on,
to watch and wait, to stay with it even when it seems
hopeless.
We still pray for the starving in many corners of
the world for whom we would like to do more to help.
We still hope for the hostages of political strife
a safe and speedy release.
we still look for peace in a world warming up for
war, though we are distressed by the insidious
aggression of evil.
And we still give what we have of our talent, time
and resource
trusting that in some small way our loyalty to love
will make a difference,
will have an impact,
will be a positive ripple in the mighty ocean of hurting people
who populate this burdened planet.
Help us, O Lord, to never give up but to keep the
faith, to trust the way of the cross, to continue
doing what we can to make a faithful difference in
this unfaithful world. Amen.

For Liberation (3)

O God of morning and heavenly light, may your Spirit
be luminous in our lives.
How grateful we are to know you.
Hear our prayers!
For those people who stand helplessly by, watching
their children swell up and die from starvation while
their government officials parlay for political and
military advantage, we ask for food to be allowed
delivery to their hungry mouths.
For those countries that are threatened by invasion
of neighboring aggressive forces, we pray for
protection and strength.
For those people near and far who are taken against
their will, held captive by force and used as currency
for stubborn demands, we pray for a speedy and non-
violent release.
For those people who have fallen victim to a sudden
illness or a violent assault,
or who are struggling with their grief and loneliness,
or who are feeling trapped by destructive
relationships,
or who are lost in their own guilt and compulsive
drives,
we pray for that liberating, loving Spirit that will
give them a new hope, a new day, a new life.
Help us to have faith enough in the power of your
resurrecting love that we can lead others to discover
the mystery of your transforming power,
the constancy of your truth and justice
and the gift of joy. Amen.

For Strangers And Enemies (1)

God of our ancestors, Lord of our lives,
you have called us to this proud land to build a home
where no one is a stranger.
You have allowed us to taste the sweet fruit of
freedom,
to enjoy worshiping you without fear of punishment
or persecution,
to speak our conscience and say what we believe
and to learn how to live with and to love people that
are different from us — people from foreign lands,
people of diverse language, custom, color.
Because you first loved us,
we have learned how to be more loving,
more compassionate, more generous.
We have learned how to be a friend to strangers,
how to care for the homeless,
how to welcome all God's children into the household
of faith.
We thank you for the courageous faith of those who
remind us what "sanctuary" means,
what faithfulness requires
and what discipleship demands.
May we continue to open our hearts and homes to the
stranger in our land, remembering that we were all
once strangers in a strange land.
And may we never grow so comfortable in this world
that we stop growing toward the world you have
designed — a world of love and justice, of sharing
and caring, of common community and uncommon joy!
Amen.

For Strangers And Enemies (2)

Seeking and Saving God,
we pray for the lost, the alienated, the embittered
and the hard-shelled.
Grant us courage to not give up on them as we remember
that you did not forsake us.
Give us compassion not to write off our enemies but
to risk reaching out to them as we remember how you
came in search for us in our darkness.
Crucified God,
who overcame power with powerlessness,
overcame death by dying
and overcame separation with forgiveness,
be our advocate and friend.
Stand by us when others stand against us;
stand for us when our knees buckle with fear and we
cannot stand for ourselves;
and stand near us when our loneliness consumes us
and we feel that no one cares.
God of death and life,
restore our unity with your Spirit and our love with
your presence. Amen.

For Peace (1)

O God of Life,
we call to you from the death that is all around us.
O God of Light,
we speak to you from the darkness within us.
We raise to you the war that rages within us,
for we are motivated by self-preservation
rather than inspired by self-sacrifice.
We follow the path of pride
rather than the highway of humility.
We listen to the gospel of greed
rather than preach the gospel of grace.
O God, grant us your peace — that peace which passes
all understanding,
that peace which can remake us and restore us as a
child of God blessed by our baptism and sacrificed
at your table to the work of reconciliation,
forgiveness, peacemaking.
Calm our fears and self-doubts,
our anxieties about tomorrow.
Still our futile attempts to secure the future by
money or military arms.
Help us, instead, O Lord, to rely on the hard work
of negotiaton, of compromise, of treaty-making,
of cooperating and tolerating nations and individuals
with whom we differ,
who anger and irritate us,
even those we would rather hurt than befriend.
Give us courage, O God, to risk our limitations in
the unlimited promise of love. Amen.

For Peace (2)

O Lord, where shall we go to find peace?
We look to the business of our lives, the work that
calls us to its activity each day and we find no peace.
We look to family and friends and discover the demands
and difficulties of mature, healthy relationships.
Where do we find your peace?
O Lord, we wish you would only take us out to green
pastures or lead us beside still waters so we may
enjoy the tranquility and solace that comes from
your Spirit. For we have found some peace in those
moments when you have called us out of the city to
a place of reflection and meditation on your
nourishing, healing word.
We would like to stay there, Lord, in flowery meadow
or quiet stream, but you lead us back to the challenge
of our existence, the demands of our society and the
human condition.
You set a table before us in the presence of our
enemies, but it is the table of sacrificial love placed
in the midst of our conflicts, our disagreements,
our confusion and disloyalty to your word and way.
O Lord, give us faith to see beyond the stress and
distraction of our earthly engagements to the
possibility of love in our lives — and so discover
the peace which abides.
O Lord of our hearts and minds, we know you are always
with us and you love us.
Grant us the peace that comes from that reassurance
so that whether we walk through fields of flowers
or strumble along streets of sadness, we will walk
beside you. Amen.

University Alumni Founders Day

We are thankful, O Lord, for the days of our lives that are
spent in your counsel and filled with wonder and mystery.
We are grateful for the curiosity you plant in young minds,
for the birth of imagination,
for the commitment to exploration and research,
for the institutions of higher learning that provide
opportunities for the expansion and enrichment of the human
spirit
and for individuals who have multiplied their knowledge into
soaring achievements.
We ask your blessing on those who support and cultivate the
means of education
and especially those bold visionaries who dare to establish
a university in the desert.
Because of the faith of these founders,
young minds will find waters of knowledge at this living well.
Thank you God, for the gift of education. Amen.

Junior High School Graduation

God of passing seasons,
as we travel from the new life of spring to the refreshment
of summer,
we ask that you walk with us through the seasons of our lives:
from childhood to adolescence,
from adolescence to young adult.
Assist us in our passage from yesterday to tomorrow.
Be with us in the confusion of transition from the familiar
to the strange.
Be with us in our terror and joy,
our dread and hope,
our looking back and looking forward.
O God of dreaming and daring,
grant us a vision of future promise
even as we celebrate the present achievement of those who have
traveled to this point in their lives.
In honoring them, we glorify the caring Spirit that has led
them to this time and place.
Thank you, God, for calling us your children even as you call
us to growth and maturity. Amen.

High School Graduation

Great God, Our Father,
let your radiant blessing shine upon this gathering today.
For we, who are tomorrow's people,
have gleaned the wisdom and knowledge of yesterday's people
and are now ready to make our mark on the road of life.
Grant us the compassion to care about human suffering, injustice
and oppression;
the intellectual discipline to search for meaningful and fair
solutions;
the courage to accept setbacks and failures;
and the faith to relentlessly pursue human decency, dignity
and integrity.
May our passage from today into tomorrow not be merely an
exercise in pomp and ceremony but rather a grateful recognition
of our heritage and a firm commitment to the world we will one
day leave behind.
May it be a little better because we walked awhile on this good
earth. Amen.

College Graduation

O God of our greatest dreams,
our highest aspirations,
we gather in the spring of our lives to await the blossoming.
The seeds of knowledge have been planted.
The ground of growth carefully cultivated.
We are prepared to bear fruit and to flower.
At this moment we look for that Spirit which enlarges the
search for knowledge to a search for truth.
We call upon that Spirit which unites the heart with the head
so that intelligence is informed by compassion and thus
transformed into wisdom.
We seek that Spirit which magnifies our ambition from what
the world can do for us to what we can do for the world.
We need the Spirit that stays with us throughout our lives
reminding us we have worth
even when we are not worthy.
O Lord of future hope,
endow this present occasion with your grace
that we may hear and believe the opportunities you have set
before us for joy. Amen.

Hospital Volunteers

Great God our Father,
we celebrate the generosity of people who hear of a concern
and respond to it.
We are thankful for those who give of their hands warmly,
who give of their hearts gladly,
who give of their time extensively.
It is fitting and timely for us to show our appreciation
to those who overlook their own schedules and turn their
attention to people in physical pain,
spiritual doubt,
emotional fear.
These are the ministers of love.
They weep with those who sorrow
and laugh with those who rejoice.
They find time to hold the hand of a lonely, forgotten person
who has been isolated by the deterioration of old age.
They find the courage to extend comfort to a small child facing
his first operation.
And they tend to all the menial, thankless tasks that are part
of a large healing institution.
We are thankful, God, that your Samaritan spirit has landed
on receptive hearts who have shown with their words and work
that they care. Amen.

Guild of Organists

Artisan of the Air,
God of Song and Spirit,
speak to us in the symphony of sound,
the hope of harmony,
the cadence of grace.
We know that where beauty abounds,
where light and color dazzle the eye,
where song fills the soul . . .
there your Spirit resides.
O Lord, teach us to listen.
May we hear in the powerful ministry of music
the struggle and suffering of life transformed by the composer,
the passion of the poet,
the love of the musician
into the rapture of your invincible presence.
Release from our hearts the agony of grief.
Heal us from the cancer of guilt.
And lift us by the sweet sound of your still, small voice
to the pinnacle of peace.
All this we ask in the name of him who taught us to sing the
song of hope and dance to the steps of victory,
our Lord Jesus Christ. Amen.

An International Balloon Festival

God of the wind and the air,
we praise you for the rising of the sun,
for this new day,
for the hope of the future.
Our spirits are lifted,
our dreams drift up into the heavens as our crafts are made
ready.
Our symphony of color will soon fill the skies
celebrating the freedom of flight,
the persistence of effort,
the courage to risk,
the human yearning for spiritual self-abandon.
We affirm your creative presence in this community,
which has dared to combine imagination, intelligence, nerve
and energy in their commitment to a common playground for people
of different nationality, color, religious view and political
persuasion.
Perhaps if we can play together
we can learn to live together with greater care and trust
and so fulfill your vision of love and forgiveness.
We pray that the balloonists and crews will return safely from
their travels so families and friends will unite in thanksgiving
for your supporting hands.
God be with us! Amen.